I'm Outta Here!

Len Woods is the pastor to collegiates at Christ Community Church in Ruston, Louisiana. He is a contributor to *The Life Application Bible for Students* and *Video Movies Worth Watching*. He is the author of *Getting Kids to Mix*.

I'M OUTTA HERE!

Facing the Tough Choices after High School

LEN WOODS

Baker Books

A Division of Baker Book House Co
Grand Rapids, Michigan 49516

Published by Baker Books
a division of Baker Book House Company
P.O. Box 6287, Grand Rapids, MI 49516-6287

Second printing, December 1995

Printed in the United States of America

Library of Congress Cataloging-in-Publication Data

Woods, Len.
    I'm outta here: facing the tough choices after high school/Len Woods.
       p.   cm.
    ISBN 0-8010-9739-8
    1. High school graduates—Conduct of life. 2. Young adults—Conduct of life. I. Title.
BJ1661.W63   1995
248.8'3—dc20   94-30385

Unless otherwise marked, Scripture quotations are from the HOLY BIBLE, NEW INTERNATIONAL VERSION ®. NIV®. Copyright © 1973, 1978, 1984 by International Bible Society. Used by permission of Zondervan Publishing House. All rights reserved.

Produced for Baker Books by the Livingstone Corporation. Dave Veerman and Michael Kendrick, project staff.

To Clayton Hays, Mike Metzger, Bill St. Cyr, Melanie McKee Barfield, Vernon Cobb, Scott Callaway, Scott Adams, Tricia Simms Duke, Greg St. Cyr, Stephen Mc-Collister, Warren Willis, Bill Newman, Pat Dunn, Charlie Schmitz, Kevin Hardy, Barkef Osigian, and *especially* Dicky and Kim Love—the magnificent assortment of mentors, friends, and roommates who encouraged me to make good choices during those years right out of high school.

CONTENTS

Contents

RELATIONSHIP CHOICES

SPIRITUAL CHOICES

INTRODUCTION

Most graduates or soon-to-be graduates receive gifts of cash, jewelry, a "senior trip," sometimes even a briefcase. Not you. You got a *book!* Some concerned parent, friend, relative, or neighbor bought it for you. And with high school in your rearview mirror and college—or perhaps a new job—just ahead, the last thing you feel like doing is reading!

I understand. But before you toss this volume aside, you need to understand a few things too. This is NOT a book of behavioral theory or deep theology. It is NOT like the obscure novels teachers made you read in English literature. (No characters named Ahab or Hawkeye or Pip! No deep symbolism! No chapter-long descriptions of the moors of Scotland in springtime!)

In fact, *I'm Outta Here!* is really not so much a book as it is a compilation of real-life stories. Inside you'll find vignettes drawn from my own college days and from the experiences of the young adults I have worked with over the last few years. Some of the situations are funny and some are incredible, but they're all based on the true adventures of real people.

Why would anyone write such a book of stories? Why would someone buy such a book . . . for *you* (especially when cash would have been so much more practical)?

Why should you bother to read these pages? Because of four facts:

1. You have certain hopes and dreams for your future, even if you can't quite articulate what those hopes and dreams are.
2. You are about to enter a fun, exciting, fulfilling, confusing, and often scary phase of life.
3. Even more than in high school, you are about to be bombarded by all sorts of conflicting opinions, ideas, and philosophies about how you should live your life.
4. You need wisdom from above if you want to make the kinds of choices that will bring lasting fulfillment.

Take some time over the next few weeks to skim these stories. After each one you'll find a few questions to get you thinking, some Bible verses to show you what God has to say about that particular issue, and, finally, a practical step or two to help you make wise decisions in your own life.

Now . . . be truthful. Doesn't a book that can do all that sound like a better graduation present than a few measly bucks (that you probably would just go spend on pizza)?

If you're still not convinced, look at it this way: You could have gotten a pen and pencil set!

A few people are wise; most are otherwise.

There are only two kinds of people who fail:
those who listen to nobody, and . . . those who
listen to everybody.

T. M. Beshere Jr.

Teach me your way, O LORD,
    and I will walk in your truth;
give me an undivided heart,
    that I may fear your name.

Psalm 86:11

The way of a fool seems right to him,
but a wise man listens to advice.

Proverbs 12:15

Integrity Issues

Is it Brandy's imagination, or have all her Christian friends completely abandoned their integrity? Some examples:

- When her campus ministry came out with a new T-shirt design, students snatched them up quickly. A few weeks later when a visitor asked about T-shirts, the group's treasurer, rather than admitting they were sold out, said, "We've got one left" and then proceeded the next day to sell the guy his own *used* shirt (at a marked up price)!
- A couple of officers in the group recently bragged about going to the movies at the mall, paying to see one film, and then staying in the theater and watching a second film for free!
- Despite firm housing rules that require overnight visitors to register with the hall director, two Christian guys have basically invited a commuting student to move in with them. He sleeps in their room at least four nights a week (and doesn't pay a cent to the college)!
- A number of friends routinely visit the new Chinese buffet near campus, pay for one dinner, and then eat off the same plate when the waitress isn't looking.
- Several guys who are really into music often borrow CDs from other people and make tapes of them so they don't have to buy their own copies.

- When someone has an out-of-town date come to campus for a football weekend, it's common for a person who is *not* going to the game to loan out his or her ID card so that the visitor won't have to buy a ticket.

Sometimes Brandy watches all these kinds of activities and thinks, *You know, I'm not trying to be legalistic or to spoil anybody's fun, but Christians are supposed to follow the rules. Just because we love Jesus and are nice people doesn't give us the right to blow off the rules that we don't like or that we think are dumb.*

But she doesn't dare say this out loud. The one time she spoke up, you'd have thought she accused her friends of being serial killers. They got *really* angry.

Thought Joggers

- As you look at your life and the lives of your Christian friends, what would you say are the most glaring "lapses in integrity"? Some of the behaviors mentioned above or other activities?
- Should Christians be held to a higher standard than non-Christians? Why or why not?
- What would non-Christians say if the actions of the Christians cited above were widely known?
- What do you think is behind this common tendency to ignore certain rules or standards?
- Have you ever felt like Brandy? What can you do in those kinds of situations?
- How can you guard against "lapses in integrity" like the ones listed above?

Eye-Openers

To encourage us to maintain a righteous character and a lifestyle of integrity (in a world that mocks honesty and right living), God gives these reminders:

Proverbs 10:9
The man of integrity walks securely,
    but he who takes crooked paths will be found out.

In other words: Those with integrity have less stress.

Proverbs 11:3
The integrity of the upright guides them,
    but the unfaithful are destroyed by their duplicity.

In other words: Those with integrity have a strong sense of what they should do.

Proverbs 28:1
The wicked man flees though no one pursues,
    but the righteous are as bold as a lion.

In other words: Those with integrity have more confidence.

Proverbs 29:6
An evil man is snared by his own sin,
    but a righteous one can sing and be glad.

In other words: Those with integrity are happier.

Life Changers

- Look up the word *integrity* in a dictionary and/or a Bible dictionary.
- Talk to a godly man or woman in your church—someone everyone considers to be a person of integrity. Ask that individual his or her secrets.
- Read the amazing story of Daniel's integrity in Daniel 6.

Moped Madness

It's a gorgeous fall day and Steven is having a blast tooling around campus on his new motor scooter. The warm sunshine and gentle breeze on his face, the feeling of freedom, pretty girls everywhere . . . *This is what college is all about*, Steven thinks to himself.

After he cruises down sorority row on University Lake Drive and traverses the parade grounds, Steven heads for Highland Dormitory. *I'll take Toni for a spin. She'll think this is the best.*

Sure enough, Toni enjoys scooting around the campus on Steven's moped. And Steven enjoys feeling her arms around him.

When Steven decides to make an illegal trip through the quadrangle, Toni protests, "Hey we're not supposed to drive through here! What if the campus police see you?"

Steven leans back and replies confidently, "Relax. If they tried to chase you on one of these things, you could get away in a flash. All you have to do is drive down the sidewalks between the buildings where their cars can't go. And then, if they tried to run after you, you'd leave them huffing and puffing behind you."

Just then Steven emerges from the quadrangle. To his shock a campus cop is sitting there in the street and begins to flag him down. Steven slows down, but his mind is whirling. *If I spin around and cut back across the quadrangle, I can lose this guy in a heartbeat.*

Toni can sense that Steven is not necessarily prepared to stop.

Thought Joggers

- Why is it that God-fearing, law-abiding people sometimes lose their senses in sticky situations?
- What do you think Toni is thinking in the story above?
- What would your friends do if they were in Steven's place? What would you do? Why?
- What are the consequences if Steven flees and evades the police?

Eye-Openers

The story of the Gibeonites, found in Joshua 9:3–26, reveals how we can mess up when we don't think, don't pray, and aren't careful.

> However, when the people of Gibeon heard what Joshua had done to Jericho and Ai, they resorted to a ruse: They went as a delegation whose donkeys were loaded with worn-out sacks and old wineskins, cracked and mended. The men put worn and patched sandals on their feet and wore old clothes. All the bread of their food supply was dry and moldy. Then they went to Joshua in the camp at Gilgal and said to him and the men of Israel, "We have come from a distant country; make a treaty with us."
>
> The men of Israel said to the Hivites, "But perhaps you live near us. How then can we make a treaty with you?"
>
> "We are your servants," they said to Joshua.

But Joshua asked, "Who are you and where do you come from?"

They answered: "Your servants have come from a very distant country because of the fame of the LORD your God. For we have heard reports of him: all that he did in Egypt, and all that he did to the two kings of the Amorites east of the Jordan—Sihon king of Heshbon, and Og king of Bashan, who reigned in Ashtaroth. And our elders and all those living in our country said to us, 'Take provisions for your journey; go and meet them and say to them, "We are your servants; make a treaty with us."' This bread of ours was warm when we packed it at home on the day we left to come to you. But now see how dry and moldy it is. And these wineskins that we filled were new, but see how cracked they are. And our clothes and sandals are worn out by the very long journey."

The men of Israel sampled their provisions but did not inquire of the LORD. Then Joshua made a treaty of peace with them to let them live, and the leaders of the assembly ratified it by oath.

Three days after they made the treaty with the Gibeonites, the Israelites heard that they were neighbors, living near them. So the Israelites set out and on the third day came to their cities: Gibeon, Kephirah, Beeroth and Kiriath Jearim. But the Israelites did not attack them, because the leaders of the assembly had sworn an oath to them by the LORD, the God of Israel.

The whole assembly grumbled against the leaders, but all the leaders answered, "We have given them our oath by the LORD, the God of Israel, and we cannot touch them now. This is what we will do to them: We will let them live, so that wrath will not fall on us for breaking the oath we swore to them." They continued, "Let them live, but let them be woodcutters and water carriers for the entire community." So the leaders' promise to them was kept.

Then Joshua summoned the Gibeonites and said, "Why did you deceive us by saying, 'We live a long way from you,' while actually you live near us? You are now under a curse: You will never cease to serve as woodcutters and water carriers for the house of my God."

They answered Joshua, "Your servants were clearly told how the LORD your God had commanded his servant Moses to give you the whole land and to wipe out all its inhabitants from before you. So we feared for our lives because of you, and that is why we did this. We are now in your hands. Do to us whatever seems good and right to you."

So Joshua saved them from the Israelites, and they did not kill them.

Life Changers

- Examine your life for areas where you are being careless or foolish. This can save you a lot of headache and heartache down the road.
- Begin reading the Proverbs for wise advice on how to live in a corrupt world.

Parking Lot Predicament

Sharon and Angie are cruising around on Thursday evening looking for something to do. There are no movies they really want to see (not even at the dollar movies), and besides, they won't get paid until tomorrow.

"You want to go to the mall?" Sharon suggests.

"I guess so. Maybe we'll see somebody hanging out in the food court."

Minutes later the girls roll into the parking lot and it's packed.

"Great!" Sharon complains. "I'm gonna have to park ten miles from the door."

"No, wait, wait. Look over there. That guy's leaving."

The girls wait a few moments, and then Sharon starts to ease into the empty space. Suddenly she stops and frowns.

"It's kind of tight."

Angie stares at her friend in disbelief. "Sharon! There's like *three feet* on either side. You could almost put a bus in there!"

"Yeah, well this car is as big as a bus."

"Oh, come on! You're cautious to the point of being an unsafe driver!"

Sharon feels stupid and so she proceeds. "Okay, but if I bonk that new Cherokee then"——screeeeeeeeech-hhhhhh!

Angie's jaw drops. Sharon's stomach sinks. The girls jump out of the car and look back at an ugly scrape in the left rear panel of the foreign car to their left. Sharon's bumper is undamaged.

"I *told* you it was close!" Sharon blurts, beginning to cry.

"You *cut it* too close!" Angie retorts.

After several minutes of Sharon's sniffling about her mom's impending anger and her sure-to-increase insurance rates, Angie makes this suggestion: "Sharon, look, nobody's around. Nobody saw you hit that car. Besides, when you look at the scrape, it's only about three inches long—maybe four. Hey, that's just a hazard of parking lots. Stuff like that happens. Look at all the dings in *your* car where people have opened their doors into you, or where shopping carts have banged into you. It's just not that big a deal. Besides, you don't even know who owns this car. I say we just get back in the car and leave."

Sharon scans the parking lot and, sure enough, there's nobody in sight. She looks at Angie as if to say, "Are you sure?"

Angie just gets back in the car.

Thought Joggers

- How do you feel when someone else messes up something of yours? What if that someone is a stranger? A friend?
- What do you think about Angie's argument? What are the possible consequences if Sharon leaves?

- What steps should Sharon take if she decides to admit her fault in this parking lot predicament?
- What are the consequences if Sharon "fesses up" to her driving mishap?
- If you walked away from an incident like the one just described, how would your conscience be affected?

Eye-Openers

Consider the biblical principles in James 4:7–10 that might apply to Sharon's situation:

> Submit yourselves, then, to God. Resist the devil, and he will flee from you. Come near to God and he will come near to you. Wash your hands, you sinners, and purify your hearts, you double-minded. Grieve, mourn and wail. Change your laughter to mourning and your joy to gloom. Humble yourselves before the Lord, and he will lift you up.

What does this passage say about temptation? What does this passage say about confession of sin? About being sorry for wrong actions?

Life Changers

- Look up the word *restitution* in a dictionary.
- Ask God to show you any unresolved situations in your own life where you need to go to another person and admit wrong.

The Gambling Game

Back during high school a few of Lance's friends bought lottery tickets every now and then. Such purchases, however, were infrequent, because the most anybody ever won was $50—and that happened only once.

Life after high school has been a different story. In the last couple of months, a number of Lance's friends have been infected by a serious case of "gambling fever." It all began one Friday when Mark, Craig, and Jason decided on the spur of the moment to visit a nearby riverboat casino. That night, Mark left town with $32 in his wallet, and he returned home with more than $700 in winnings! Not surprisingly, the next weekend *two carloads* of friends returned, hoping to duplicate Mark's success in blackjack, or perhaps hit the jackpot in slots.

Two consecutive money-losing excursions convinced the group to try their hand at a new game. So *now* the plan is this: This weekend, a few folks want to venture over to Capital Downs and put some money on the ponies.

Says Craig, "My dad told me how to do it. He showed me a way to hedge your bet. We can't really lose, and we just might hit it big."

The guys are urging Lance to join them. "C'mon, Lance! You missed out on all the fun we had at the riverboat."

Lance is skeptical. "Yeah, right! I missed out on a chance to blow all my hard-earned money."

"Or," Mark retorts, "maybe a chance to make some easy money."

"Look, guys, I'm saving for college. I can't afford to throw money away like that."

Jason shakes his head violently. "No, man, you've got it all wrong. Stop looking at it like you're throwing money away. Think of it as *entertainment* . . . like going out to eat and to a movie. If you did that, you'd spend *at least* $20. And what would you have at the end of the evening? Nothing. So, do this. Put that same amount of money in your pocket Friday—$25 or $30—and come with us to the track. If you bet and don't win a thing, you still have fun and it's no big loss. But if you pick a *winner*, you come out way ahead. That's the way you've got to look at it."

Lance has never looked at it that way. Suddenly, he's reconsidering his decision not to join his friends.

Thought Joggers

- Why, in your opinion, has gambling exploded in popularity in this country?
- What forms of gambling do your friends, family, or relatives participate in and why?
- What do you think of Jason's argument?
- What are the potential problems with becoming a recreational gambler?
- What would you likely do in Lance's situation?

Eye-Openers

The Bible does not *condemn* gambling outright, but it does provide us with these insights:

1 Timothy 6:7–11

For we brought nothing into the world, and we can take nothing out of it. But if we have food and clothing, we will be content with that. People who want to get rich fall into temptation and a trap and into many foolish and harmful desires that plunge men into ruin and destruction. For the love of money is a root of all kinds of evil. Some people, eager for money, have wandered from the faith and pierced themselves with many griefs.

But you, man of God, flee from all this, and pursue righteousness, godliness, faith, love, endurance and gentleness.

In other words: The desire for instant wealth is dangerous.

1 Corinthians 6:12

"Everything is permissible for me"—but not everything is beneficial. "Everything is permissible for me"—but I will not be mastered by anything.

In other words: We are to be careful not to get involved in activities that become all-consuming.

Matthew 6:31–33

So do not worry, saying, "What shall we eat?" or "What shall we drink?" or "What shall we wear?" For the pagans run after all these things, and your heavenly Father knows that you need them. But seek first his kingdom and his righteousness, and all these things will be given to you as well.

In other words: When we follow Christ, he promises to meet all our material needs.

Life Changers

- Before you spend even a *dollar* on any form of legalized gambling, spend a few minutes in the library researching the odds of winning such games of chance. Statistics prove that you stand a far greater chance of getting hit by lightning than you do of winning big money through gambling.
- Urge your friends who gamble to redirect some of that "discretionary income" towards helping sponsor an underprivileged third-world child. You can "adopt" a child for $20–$30 a month through groups like Compassion International or World Vision.
- Ask God to protect you from potentially addictive behaviors.
- If you think you might have a gambling problem, contact your local chapter of Gamblers Anonymous. They are usually listed in the Yellow Pages.

Beating the System

After six parking violations (at $10 a pop!), B. J. decided he would *never again* get a ticket. So he finally registered his vehicle and made a commitment to begin parking in the approved white zones, right? Wrong. He took a used parking ticket, scanned it into his computer, deleted the handwritten parts, and printed out a dozen almost-perfect replicas. He reasoned this way: "Whenever I park, I'll just fill out one of these babies and stick it under my wiper. Then, when the traffic patrol comes by, they'll see a ticket already on my windshield, and they'll keep going."

The plan worked . . . for awhile. But one day his fake ticket was gone, and in its place was a "new" ticket. So B. J. devised a more complicated plan. He grabbed his camera, found a professor's car in one of the remote parking lots, and took a picture of its faculty parking sticker. When he developed the film and cut the snapshot down to size, he suddenly had his very own faculty parking permit! Affixing that fake sticker to his rear bumper, B. J. thought he was set.

However, because of the confiscated fake ticket, the campus authorities were waiting for him. Yesterday, he returned to his car after class only to find a police "boot" attached to the front tire.

Suddenly B. J. is in big trouble. The campus police chief and the dean of students have been using words and phrases like "fraud," "criminal intent," and "disciplinary suspension." Complicating the whole situation is the fact that B. J. is already on probation for a similar beat-the-system scheme about a year ago!

Thought Joggers

- What is the motivation behind the desire to beat the system?
- Why is it that we hate rules and regulations that tell us what we can and cannot do?
- If you had been aware of B. J.'s plan and he were a good friend of yours, would you have discouraged him from following through on his scheme to beat the system? Why or why not?
- Why do you think B. J. didn't learn from his first failed attempt to beat the system? What do you think lies ahead for him?

Eye-Openers

The Book of Proverbs clearly outlines the difference between a wise person and a foolish person:

Proverbs 10:23
A fool finds pleasure in evil conduct,
    but a man of understanding delights in wisdom.

Proverbs 12:15
The way of a fool seems right to him,
    but a wise man listens to advice.

Proverbs 13:16
Every prudent man acts out of knowledge,
    but a fool exposes his folly.

Proverbs 14:16
A wise man fears the LORD and shuns evil,
  but a fool is hotheaded and reckless.

Proverbs 17:10
A rebuke impresses a man of discernment
  more than a hundred lashes a fool.

Proverbs 26:11–12
As a dog returns to its vomit,
  so a fool repeats his folly.
Do you see a man wise in his own eyes?
  There is more hope for a fool than for him.

Proverbs 28:26
He who trusts in himself is a fool,
  but he who walks in wisdom is kept safe.

Life Changers

- There is an old country saying that admonishes us to "Go to school off your friends." The meaning is this: Learn from the poor choices and mistakes of others. Don't repeat their folly. By watching them you can save yourself a lot of grief!
- Beware of the lure of pragmatism. Pragmatism is that philosophy that says, "Whatever works is what is right." For example, some people break the rules, never get caught, and pragmatically reason, "Well, my plan worked; therefore, this is the way to live." That's not only wrong thinking, it is foolish and destructive as well!

College or Not?

No one realizes it, but Stacy is suffering from a severe case of "Senior Panic."

From all outer appearances she's sitting pretty. She's been accepted to a state school about three hours from her home (the university her parents attended). She's been promised a good bit of financial aid, and she's got the inside track on a decent campus job. Plus, if she wants to go through rush, she's pretty much guaranteed a bid to join Kappa Gamma Phi, a social sorority. (Her mom is an alum.)

But the inner reality is that Stacy is confused and worried. Despite the fact that college seems to be falling into place for her, Stacy isn't terribly motivated to go. The thought of classes and lectures and research papers turns her stomach. Yet because she was a B student in high school (and she did especially well in English), her parents are convinced she needs to pursue higher education (possibly a degree in education).

It's likely that Stacy is confused because of what happened just before prom a few weeks ago. She cut and styled the hair of a couple of friends, and the results were amazing. Other classmates marveled at her ability and have been making appointments to get *their* hair done. All this has Stacy thinking that what she'd *really* enjoy doing with her life is to cut and style hair—and maybe one day even have her own shop.

But she doesn't dare tell her parents that. They seem

to think that college is a necessity, and they'd be terribly disappointed if Stacy didn't go.

Thought Joggers

- In your opinion, who should go to college and why?
- Put yourself in Stacy's situation. What would you do? What could she say to her parents to help them understand her feelings and concerns?
- What factors led to your decision to either go to college or not?
- Forget the money! What job would you really enjoy doing in life?

Eye-Openers

First Corinthians 12 demonstrates the truth that God designed each one of us for a different purpose. (Though the passage really refers to how Christians function within the *church*, the underlying principle applies to all of life.) We should never feel inferior to another, nor should we strive to be something we are not.

All these are the work of one and the same Spirit, and he gives them to each one, just as he determines.

The body is a unit, though it is made up of many parts; and though all its parts are many, they form one body. So it is with Christ. For we were all baptized by one Spirit into one body—whether Jews or Greeks, slave or free—and we were all given the one Spirit to drink.

Now the body is not made up of one part but of many. If the foot should say, "Because I am not a hand, I do not belong to the body," it would not for that reason cease to be part of the body. And if the ear should say, "Because I am not an eye, I do not belong to the body," it would not for that reason cease to be part of the body. If the whole body were an eye, where would the sense of hearing be? If the whole body were an ear, where would the sense of smell be? But in fact God has arranged the parts in the body, every one of them, just as he wanted them to be. If they were all one part, where would the body be? As it is, there are many parts, but one body.

The eye cannot say to the hand, "I don't need you!" And the head cannot say to the feet, "I don't need you!" On the contrary, those parts of the body that seem to be weaker are indispensable, and the parts that we think are less honorable we treat with special honor. And the parts that are unpresentable are treated with special modesty, while our presentable parts need no special treatment. But God has combined the members of the body and has given greater honor to the parts that lacked it, so that there should be no division in the body, but that its parts should have equal concern for each other. If one part suffers, every part suffers with it; if one part is honored, every part rejoices with it.

Life Changers

- Ask God to show you what you are good at and what he has created you to do.
- Visit your school guidance counselor and ask him or her to give you an aptitude exam or career profile. Such a test can help determine your natural strengths and abilities, and it can save you the trouble of ending up in a major or a job you really don't enjoy.

Cheating Schemes

Rachel saw some creative cheating her senior year, but compared to what she has witnessed her first semester in college, high school was the minor leagues! Some examples follow:

- A certain geology professor posts the answers to his exams on a bulletin board outside the classroom on test days so that students can check their answers and know their scores before they even leave the building. Rachel heard through the grapevine that one student with longer hair wore an earphone during a recent exam and had a buddy stationed outside the room (at the bulletin board) in order to radio the correct answers to him!
- Most fraternities and sororities keep huge filing cabinets of old tests (including some stolen exams) and used speeches so that their members can "maintain appropriate levels of academic excellence."
- One enterprising student has a massive collection of *Quickie Classics* and dozens of literary works on video that he rents out to fellow students. He's making a killing for obvious reasons. Watching *The Red Badge of Courage* or reading a brief summary of *Animal Farm* is much easier than actually reading the books.

- Numerous students routinely pay $15–$25 for research or term papers that are sold by a mail-order company on the East Coast.

Sometimes Rachel looks around and thinks, *Everybody on this campus is cheating! That's why they have all this free time to goof off and have fun, and I'm locked away in some study carrel in the library. It ticks me off! Why am I killing myself to play by the rules when no one else does?*

Thought Joggers

- How widespread was cheating in your high school? Why do you think?
- In many cases, cheaters are like shoplifters. They don't really *need* to break the rules. In the same way that many shoplifters often have the money to buy what they have taken, many cheaters have the intelligence to do well on their own. How do you explain this phenomenon?
- There's a familiar old saying that goes, "When you cheat, you only cheat yourself." Do you agree with that statement? Why or why not?
- How can Christian students resist the urge to cheat when the practice is so prevalent?
- Have you ever felt like Rachel? What did you do?

Eye-Openers

For those who must live in the midst of a dishonest, unethical academic environment (and who are tempted to join in the deception), God gives these reminders:

Psalm 32:2
Blessed is the man
    whose sin the LORD does not count against him
    and in whose spirit is no deceit.

In other words: God blesses those who refrain from deceitful practices.

Proverbs 12:20–22
There is deceit in the hearts of those who plot evil,
    but joy for those who promote peace.
No harm befalls the righteous,
    but the wicked have their fill of trouble.
The LORD detests lying lips,
    but he delights in men who are truthful.

In other words: Joy and peace are the property of those who resist the urge to cheat.

Titus 1:7
Since an overseer is entrusted with God's work, he must be blameless—not overbearing, not quick-tempered, not given to drunkenness, not violent, not pursuing dishonest gain.

In other words: Those who would be Christian leaders must turn away from dishonest gain (which is another way to describe cheating).

Life Changers

- Realize this: Most cheating schemes involve tremendous energy, effort, and time to implement.

The point? In the time it takes to plan and pull off a cheating scheme, you could go ahead and study and actually do the work! (And you'd be free from the worry of getting caught!)

- Pray for the integrity to live as you should. Remember that an honest life is a powerful witness.

Class Confusion

Shelly has hit on a scheduling scheme that pays pretty good dividends. Each semester, she signs up for one class too many. After her dad pays her fees for tuition, room, and board, Shelly goes to all her classes for a couple of weeks. She then decides which one will be the hardest. Shelly drops that course just before the final drop date, pockets about $150 in refunds, and her transcript is spared the trauma of a bad grade.

It never occurs to Shelly that she ought to inform her dad of her "class dropping" and send him the refunds. She just figures she's being smart to avoid difficult courses and to get back at least *some* of her tuition.

In a separate but related issue, Shelly also has gotten into the habit of skipping a lot of classes. She reasons, "Hey, *I'm* the one paying *them* for an education. When you think about it, I'm like a customer. If I don't feel like coming, or if a particular teacher is boring, why should I have to endure that? I ought to have the right to do what I want. As long as I get the notes and do the work, what difference does it make? Besides, I can sit at home and read the textbook and get more out of that than I could *ever* get out of a lecture!"

Wonder what Shelly's dad would say if he knew about her dropping and skipping of classes?

Thought Joggers

- Do you think most students go to college to get an education or to get a degree? What's the difference?

39

- What is the best way to learn—listening to lectures, reading textbooks, or getting hands-on experience? Why?
- What would you do to improve higher education in this country?
- How do you think a potential employer might react if he or she saw a transcript with lots of "dropped courses" indicated? Would it make a difference? Why or why not?
- What about Shelly's argument that as a student, she's like a consumer, that it's her education, and that she should be able to attend when she feels like it? Should schools be able to require that students attend class? Why or why not?
- Evaluate Shelly's behavior. Is she taking full advantage of her chance to get a college education? What counsel would you give her and why?

Eye-Openers

In Bible terminology a steward is a person who has been given a trust and who is expected to wisely care for that thing or situation or responsibility that has been granted to him or her. See how these principles and passages might apply to Shelly's situation:

1 Corinthians 9:17
If I preach voluntarily, I have a reward; if not voluntarily, I am simply discharging the trust committed to me.

In other words: As a preacher, Paul had an obligation to share the gospel.

1 Corinthians 4:2
Now it is required that those who have been given a trust must prove faithful.

Ephesians 5:15
Be very careful, then, how you live—not as unwise but as wise, making the most of every opportunity, because the days are evil.

In other words: We must be faithful with whatever opportunities God gives us.

Life Changers

- If you have been accepted at a university or college, count your blessings. The great majority of the people in the world never get the opportunity to pursue higher education. Don't squander your opportunity to learn and grow!
- The same principle applies if you are working or if you are going into one of the armed services. Take advantage of every situation that comes your way. Don't just float through life like so many people, doing just enough to "get by." Seize every opportunity!
- Read the parable of the servants in Matthew 25:14–30.

Dormitory Rules

Everybody in Adams Hall knows "the big three" dorm rules: (1) No more than six people in any room at one time; (2) No visitors of the opposite sex after midnight; and (3) No overnight visitors without written permission from the director of housing.

Everybody *knows* those rules, but few people follow them. The RAs (resident advisors) on each floor are often too busy with other responsibilities to monitor the comings and goings of dozens of guests.

Last night Jeremy and Ray invited several friends over to their room in Adams Hall to eat pizza and watch some videos. They were having so much fun they quickly lost track of time. When the party finally broke up at 2:20 A.M., the guys decided to try to sneak their female visitors out the south entrance. Tiptoeing quietly down the darkened hallway, the group rounded a corner and ran right into Chris, the hall director.

Jeremy and Ray immediately began making excuses. Chris listened patiently, and finally said, "Guys, I know it was an innocent mistake, and I know you weren't trying to cause trouble, but I've warned you before about the curfew. I can't keep looking the other way. I'm going to have to deny your visitors privileges for a week."

Jeremy and Ray immediately were struck by the same thought: "But it's Parents Weekend! How are we going to tell our families tomorrow morning that they can't even visit our room?"

Eye-Openers

Consider the principles found in these passages from Titus that apply to life on the campus or life on the job:

Titus 2:6–15

Similarly, encourage the young men to be self-controlled. In everything set them an example by doing what is good. In your teaching show integrity, seriousness and soundness of speech that cannot be condemned, so that those who oppose you may be ashamed because they have nothing bad to say about us.

Teach slaves to be subject to their masters in everything, to try to please them, not to talk back to them, and not to steal from them, but to show that they can be fully trusted, so that in every way they will make the teaching about God our Savior attractive.

For the grace of God that brings salvation has appeared to all men. It teaches us to say "No" to ungodliness and worldly passions, and to live self-controlled, upright and godly lives in this present age, while we wait for the blessed hope—the glorious appearing of our great God and Savior, Jesus Christ, who gave himself for us to redeem us from all wickedness and to purify for himself a people that are his very own, eager to do what is good.

These, then, are the things you should teach. Encourage and rebuke with all authority. Do not let anyone despise you.

Titus 3:1–2
Remind the people to be subject to rulers and authorities, to be obedient, to be ready to do whatever is good, to slander no one, to be peaceable and considerate, and to show true humility toward all men.

Life Changers

- Take a few minutes to mentally list the various rules and regulations that you are expected to follow in all the areas of your life. Evaluate how well you are submitting to the authorities that God has placed over you.
- Ask God to give you the wisdom to see the value of rules and the humility to follow even the ones that seem silly.

Giving In to a Goof-Off

Hillary hangs up the phone.

"Who was that?" inquires Kellie.

"Rob."

"Rob *Richardson?*"

"Yep."

"Omigosh. He's the cutest guy on campus! What did he want?"

"To come study with me."

Kellie is shocked. "No way! I don't believe it!"

"I don't either," Hillary replies, her voice dripping with sarcasm.

"Hillary, why aren't you excited? I'd be screaming!"

"Look, Kellie. Rob could care less about me. He just wants my history notes."

"How do you know?"

"Because he's a total goof-off when it comes to school."

"Why do you say that?"

"Because it's true. He almost never comes to class. And if by chance he does bother to show up, he falls asleep or he flirts or he reads magazines. And so now, here we are the night before the first big test. Basically, he wants me to teach him four weeks of material in one night."

"What are you gonna do?"

"I'm thinking about telling him to get lost!"

"Hillary, this is *Rob Richardson* you're talking about!"

"So? I'm sick of lazy goof-offs like Rob using and abusing me. If I can get my tail out of bed and go to class every morning and listen to the lectures and take notes, so can he!"

Kellie is surprised at the strong reaction of her friend.

Thought Joggers

- What type of person are you? The kind who would have to borrow the notes of another or the kind who would be asked by others to borrow your notes? Why do you think you are this way?
- What do you think about Hillary's attitude? Why?
- Is there anything unethical, illegal, or sinful about what Rob is doing or not doing? Explain your answer.
- Where is the line between helping another student and "carrying" another student?
- Assuming Hillary decides not to help Rob, how might she express her feelings without coming across as judgmental and harsh?

Eye-Openers

Consider these Bible passages and principles which provide insight for the situation in which Hillary finds herself:

Proverbs 14:23
All hard work brings a profit,
 but mere talk leads only to poverty.

In other words: God blesses those who work hard.

2 Thessalonians 3:6–7
In the name of the Lord Jesus Christ, we command you, brothers, to keep away from every brother who is idle and does not live according to the teaching you received from us. For you yourselves know how you ought to follow our example. We were not idle when we were with you.

In other words: We are to steer clear of idle people.

2 Thessalonians 3:10
For even when we were with you, we gave you this rule: "If a man will not work, he shall not eat."

In other words: Lazy people are not to be granted a free ride.

Life Changers

- Examine your own habits. What is your reputation? Do people look at you as a lazy person who uses and abuses others and seeks a free ride?
- If you have friends who always want to borrow notes, rather than just loaning out your work (and enabling them to continue in a lifestyle of laziness), offer to help them learn better study skills.
- Pray for the compassion to help the truly needy, the courage to confront the truly lazy, and the wisdom to recognize the difference.

Home or Away?

Randy is facing a big dilemma: Should he attend the state school located in his hometown or go to college 150 miles away in a neighboring state?

Here's his pro-con worksheet:

Central State	Bunkie College
+ Lower tuition and living costs	+ Outstanding academic reputation
+ Familiar surroundings	+ The major I really want—biomedical engineering
+ Lots of friends	+ Chance to get out on my own
+ Scholarship possible	− Would have to take out student loans and would be in debt when I'm done with school
− Parents pushing for this	
− Big, impersonal school	+ Smaller school
− Located in a smaller town	+ Life in the big city—more to do!
− Would probably never get my own car	+ Might get to buy a car!

As you can probably tell from Randy's list, he's leaning toward Bunkie College. So what's the problem? This: His parents keep talking about the money factor. They keep talking about the danger of going into debt, and they keep making comments like, "Well, if you went to Central, you could always live at home."

That thought drives Randy up the wall. Deep down inside he feels like his mom is trying to make him feel guilty. He feels somewhat manipulated and controlled and pressured, yet the thought of having to pay back a big student loan isn't too appealing to him.

Thought Joggers

- When it comes to making big decisions, do you tend to agonize and analyze, or do you quickly choose a course of action and move on? Why do you think you make decisions the way you do?
- In addition to making out a pro-con worksheet, what else could Randy do to figure out the proper course of action?
- How can children honor their parents and yet also establish a healthy level of independence?
- What advice would you give Randy?
- What would you say to Randy's parents if they asked your opinion?

Eye-Openers

Consider a couple of Bible passages and principles that refer to knowing the will of God:

Psalm 32:8
I will instruct you and teach you in the way you
   should go; I will counsel you and watch over you.

In other words: God promises to give us guidance.

Acts 20:22
And now, compelled by the Spirit, I am going to Jerusalem, not knowing what will happen to me there.

Romans 8:14
Because those who are led by the Spirit of God are sons of God.

In other words: When we are willing to do God's will, whatever that might entail, we experience God's leading.

Life Changers

- A good general rule to knowing God's will is this: If after praying and consulting both the Scriptures and godly Christian advisors you feel *led* to do a certain thing, chances are good that course of action is the will of God. If, however, you feel *pressured* and *uneasy* about following a certain course of action, you should stop and reexamine your direction.
- A number of good books are available on the subject of how to know God's will. Ask your pastor or youth leader to recommend one for you to read.

Parental Pressure

In both his junior and senior years, Danny was an all-district high school basketball player. He had hoped for a scholarship to play major college ball, but it just wasn't to be—maybe if he were a little quicker and about four inches taller.

Danny's parents won't let it die. They think he's throwing away a chance for some free education. Tonight his dad is at it again: "Okay, maybe you can't play in a *big program*, but what about small college ball, or even junior college ball? A lot of coaches would *die* for a shooter like you. You don't turn the ball over and you have excellent fundamentals."

Danny looks at his dad like he's listening, but inside he's thinking, *I'm also five foot nine, and I weigh 140 pounds.*

Danny's dad continues the speech he's given a dozen times. "Son, I know what you are capable of doing. If you put your mind to it, you could go to a lot of schools and make the team as a walk-on. Maybe you wouldn't get a scholarship the first year, but if you busted your tail, I guarantee you'd win one by your sophomore year."

Danny nods, but inside he's thinking, *What if I'm tired of busting my tail? What if I just don't want the hassle of organized sports—all the practices and workouts, and the pressure? It was okay for high school, but now I'd really just enjoy going to school and working and having a social life.*

"Think about it. Okay, Son? It would really help your mom and me financially if you could get some sort of scholarship."

Thought Joggers

- If you could wave a magic wand and make changes in the way you relate to your parents, what changes would you make?
- What expectations do your parents have for you?
- What dreams or goals do you have for yourself?
- Who's wrong? Danny, for "not being a good steward of his abilities," or his parents, for pressuring him to do something he doesn't really want to do?
- What should Danny do?

Eye-Openers

The following Scriptures offer practical principles for those who find themselves in a situation similar to Danny's:

Exodus 20:12
Honor your father and your mother, so that you may live long in the land the LORD your God is giving you.

In other words: God expects us to honor our parents.

Luke 14:26
If anyone comes to me and does not hate his father and mother, his wife and children, his brothers and sisters—yes, even his own life—he cannot be my disciple.

In other words: Our ultimate devotion should be to God and to doing his will.

Life Changers

- If you have parents who are pushing you or pressuring you to do something you are not comfortable doing, seek advice from your pastor or youth leader.
- In the life of Jesus, there were several occasions in which he seemingly went against the wishes of his earthly parents because of his higher commitment to do the will of his heavenly Father (Luke 2:48–50; John 2:1–5; Matt. 12:46–50; Mark 3:21).
- We sometimes forget that our parents are people too—that they have hopes and dreams and fears just like us. A lot of times we are ticked *at* or frustrated *with* our parents because we've never taken the time to really listen to them and understand where they're coming from. Take an evening (at least one) before you leave home and ask your parents all about their lives. Find out about their own upbringing, about their parents, about their teenage and college years. Knowing *how* they got to where they are will give you insight into *why* they are the way they are.

Plagiarism

If Rod could physically manage it, he'd give himself a giant kick in the rump. Why? Because it's 4:30 Thursday afternoon. That means in exactly sixteen hours he's expected to hand his sociology instructor a typed, thirty-page paper on "The Changing Culture of Australian Aborigines in the Twentieth Century." Except for checking out a handful of books and photocopying a few journal, magazine, and encyclopedia articles, Rod has not even *started* his project.

At 5:18 he's still staring at a mostly blank computer screen. Charles, a friend who lives next door, enters the room.

"How's it coming along?"

Rod doesn't even look up. "It *isn't!*"

"So what's the problem?"

"The *problem* is I don't even know where to begin. I don't know how to organize this thing. I can't even begin to understand all the psycho-babble in these books. Basically I'm clueless. . . . And I'm in *big* trouble!"

Charles smiles, shakes his head, and grabs a few of the articles on Rod's desk. "Look, you're thinking too hard. Haven't you ever done a paper before? Just copy bits and pieces from all these sources. Take a paragraph or two from here, a sentence from there, then slap some goofy conclusion on it. You know, the kind of ending where you make it sound like writing this paper is the greatest thing you've ever done in your whole life. I'm telling you, that's all there is to it. Do that, and you'll get at least a C—maybe even a B."

"Just copy from all these sources?"

"That's what *I* do."

"Isn't that plagiarism?"

"No! If you copy it all from one source, *that's* plagiarism. Copy from a whole bunch of sources, and it's called *research*."

"Are you sure?"

"Hey, man, you're talking to a guy who's been doing it for two years. I'm telling you, it works!"

All of a sudden, Rod feels invigorated.

Thought Joggers

- Besides writing papers, what are some other circumstances where people are tempted to borrow ideas or take credit for work that was really done by others?
- What do you think of Charles' definitions of *plagiarism* and *research*?
- Is it okay to copy other people as long as you put their words in quotation marks? Why or why not?
- How might Rod have avoided this situation where he is tempted to indulge in plagiarism?
- What other options besides plagiarism does Rod have?

Eye-Openers

Consider the character demonstrated by Shadrach, Meshach, and Abednego in Daniel 3. They could have compromised and avoided getting into trouble. Instead they did the right thing and trusted God with the result:

At this time some astrologers came forward and denounced the Jews. They said to King Nebuchadnezzar, "O king, live forever! You have issued a decree, O king, that everyone who hears the sound of the horn, flute, zither, lyre, harp, pipes and all kinds of music must fall down and worship the image of gold, and that whoever does not fall down and worship will be thrown into a blazing furnace. But there are some Jews whom you have set over the affairs of the province of Babylon— Shadrach, Meshach and Abednego—who pay no attention to you, O king. They neither serve your gods nor worship the image of gold you have set up."

Furious with rage, Nebuchadnezzar summoned Shadrach, Meshach and Abednego. So these men were brought before the king, and Nebuchadnezzar said to them, "Is it true, Shadrach, Meshach and Abednego, that you do not serve my gods or worship the image of gold I have set up? Now when you hear the sound of the horn, flute, zither, lyre, harp, pipes and all kinds of music, if you are ready to fall down and worship the image I made, very good. But if you do not worship it, you will be thrown immediately into a blazing furnace. Then what god will be able to rescue you from my hand?"

Shadrach, Meshach and Abednego replied to the king, "O Nebuchadnezzar, we do not need to defend ourselves before you in this matter. If we are thrown into the blazing furnace, the God we serve is able to save us from it, and he will rescue us from your hand, O king. But even if he does not, we want you to know, O king, that we will not serve your gods or worship the image of gold you have set up."

Life Changers

- Most colleges and universities have strict rules (with devastating consequences) against plagiarism. Make sure you read your school's code of student conduct.
- The next time you are given a big assignment, break it down into manageable chunks. Accomplishing a little bit every day can keep you out of those terrible situations where you have to do it all in one night.
- Take a month to read the book of Proverbs. (It has thirty-one chapters, so you just have to read one chapter a day.)

The Housing Scam

Celeste Clandean, an eighteen-year-old freshman-to-be at Canyon Creek College, is in the middle of an annoying, frustrating, confusing, bureaucratic predicament. Here are the facts:

1. University rules state that all first- and second-year students *must* either live at home or on campus; but . . .
2. Celeste has *no desire* to live in a dormitory on campus; one possible alternative is that . . .
3. Celeste's parents live only thirty miles from the campus; however . . .
4. Celeste doesn't want to commute; furthermore . . .
5. Celeste is a *very* responsible, disciplined student; and the bottom line is . . .
6. Celeste *really* wants to get an apartment near campus; but . . .
7. The only way Celeste can get an apartment is if she tells the university she is actually living at home and commuting; that would be lying; however . . .
8. Celeste's parents don't mind telling the school she'll be commuting (they rationalize that she will be coming home most weekends) because they agree with her that the school's housing regulations are stupid; and yet . . .

9. Despite the fact that Celeste seems to have everything worked out for circumventing the university's housing policy, she feels uneasy writing on her application that she'll be commuting.

Thought Joggers

- What, in your opinion, are the reasons that some schools require students to live on campus?
- Since Celeste has her parents' approval to tell the university she'll be commuting, why do you suppose she feels uneasy about filling out the necessary application?
- What rules or laws do you obey selectively? Why?
- What regulations do you follow without fail?
- What does it communicate to children when they see their own parents distort the truth?
- If you were a friend of the Clandean family and you knew about their plans, what, if anything, would you say?

Eye-Openers

Consider these Bible passages and principles:

John 8:44

You belong to your father, the devil, and you want to carry out your father's desire. He was a murderer from the beginning, not holding to the truth, for there is no truth in him. When he lies, he speaks his native language, for he is a liar and the father of lies.

In other words: Deception is a devilish trait.

Psalm 31:5
Into your hands I commit my spirit;
  redeem me, O LORD, the God of truth.

Titus 1:2
... a faith and knowledge resting on the hope of eternal life, which God, who does not lie, promised before the beginning of time.

In other words: Honesty is a divine quality.

The bottom line? When we practice deception, we act more like the devil and less like God.

Life Changers

- Ask God to shine the spotlight of his truth into your heart and life. Ask him to reveal areas or situations or relationships in which you are being deceptive or misleading. Confess your dishonesty and ask for the strength to be a man or woman of integrity.
- Commit together with a Christian friend that you will both be completely truthful in your dealings with others. Hold each other accountable. Look up the words *truthful, true, truth, honesty, honest,* and *sincerity* in a Bible concordance. Note what you find.

Time Management

Though she is in her third week of college, Kris still can't get over how great it is. No parents nagging her to clean her room, the opportunity to eat *whatever* she wants *whenever* she feels like it, the freedom to come and go without having to "report" her whereabouts—it's no wonder Kris walks about the campus in a kind of a dreamy trance.

She's discovering lots of other benefits to college life as well: social events, tons of people to do things with, and the intramural complex (sort of the ultimate health club!). But the one thing that surprises Kris most is all the free time she has. She only goes to class from 8:15 to 11:45 on Mondays, Wednesdays, and Fridays. Her afternoons are free! On Tuesdays and Thursdays, the schedule is even better—one class from 12:15 to 1:45! And get this—most of her professors give only two or three exams each semester. No daily assignments—just reading and listening to lectures. Only one instructor has assigned a research paper.

Even when you crank in her work schedule—about fifteen hours a week answering the phone in the engineering department—Kris is far less busy than she was in high school. So she's been staying up late, taking lots of naps, and hanging out with all her new friends. She's even skipped several classes, reasoning, *I can always get the notes from someone.*

Kris doesn't realize it yet, but she's not managing her time very well. She's having a good time now and not thinking long-term. And like so many other college freshmen, when midterms hit in a few weeks, Kris is going to be in for a major shock!

Thought Joggers

- Why do you think some people thrive in highly structured settings while others do well in settings where there is little structure?
- Why do you suppose high schools keep students in class about thirty-five to forty hours a week when colleges only require about fifteen to twenty class or lab hours weekly?
- How would you rate your time management skills? Explain your rating.
- What could you do, or whom could you talk to, to improve your time management skills?
- What do you think lies ahead for Kris?

Eye-Openers

The following Scriptures offer wise advice and helpful principles for those who need to learn time management:

Psalm 90:12
Teach us to number our days aright,
   that we may gain a heart of wisdom.

In other words: We need to recognize the fleeting nature of time.

Ecclesiastes 3:1–8
There is a time for everything, and a season for every
activity under heaven:
  a time to be born and a time to die,
  a time to plant and a time to uproot,
  a time to kill and a time to heal,
  a time to tear down and a time to build,
  a time to weep and a time to laugh,
  a time to mourn and a time to dance,
  a time to scatter stones and a time to gather them,
  a time to embrace and a time to refrain,
  a time to search and a time to give up,
  a time to keep and a time to throw away,
  a time to tear and a time to mend,
  a time to be silent and a time to speak,
  a time to love and a time to hate,
  a time for war and a time for peace.

In other words: God gives us time to do everything that
needs to be done.

Proverbs 16:3
Commit to the LORD whatever you do,
  and your plans will succeed.

In other words: When we put God first, we can be successful.

Life Changers

- Track your use of time for one week. See exactly
  how much time you spend sleeping, going to meetings, studying, reading, watching TV, socializing,
  eating, commuting, shopping, praying, attending

church, exercising, etc. Tally up the results, subtract the total from 168 (the number of hours in a week), and you'll be able to see where you are wasting time (or not spending enough time).

- Ask your parents or youth leader for a good book on time management. Read it and discuss it with a friend.

Credit Card Craze

This afternoon when Keith checked his mailbox, he found a pleasant surprise—a letter from a bank in New Jersey offering him a pre-approved, no-fee Visa card with a $1000 credit line.

Keith can't believe it. He calls his sister Kate (who's older and married). "You mean, all I have to do is fill out this application and send it in, and they'll send me a credit card?"

"Yeah, that's pretty much it. But Keith, before you get too excited, let me warn you—credit cards can get you in *big* trouble."

"How?"

"Well, it feels pretty good to go into a store and slap down that plastic and walk out with something you want. It's painless. But then the bill comes, and all your little charges—$25 here, $40 there—they add up quick."

"So?"

"So most people can't pay off their balance, and so they get in this trap of just making the minimum payment. They end up paying hundreds of dollars in interest, and they never get out of debt."

"Yeah, but that's dumb. I would never make that mistake."

"That's what everybody says, but I'm telling you, having a credit card can be addictive—and destructive. Keith, if I were you, before I signed or mailed anything, I'd talk to Dad."

"No way! If I talk to him, he'll tell me not to do it."

"Well, then, maybe you *shouldn't* do it."

"I don't know. I'll think about it. Thanks for the advice."

Keith hangs up the phone, stares at the application, and thinks about how great it would be to have his own credit card.

Thought Joggers

- Why do you think merchants and banks often target 18–22-year-olds for credit and charge card appeals?
- What are the pros and cons of having a credit card?
- What advice would you give Keith?
- What (honestly) do you think you'd do in a similar situation? Why?

Eye-Openers

When thinking through the credit card question, remember these principles:

Romans 13:7–8

Give everyone what you owe him: If you owe taxes, pay taxes; if revenue, then revenue; if respect, then respect; if honor, then honor.

Let no debt remain outstanding, except the continuing debt to love one another, for he who loves his fellowman has fulfilled the law.

Matthew 6:19–21

Do not store up for yourselves treasures on earth, where moth and rust destroy, and where thieves break in and steal. But store up for yourselves treasures in heaven, where moth and rust do not destroy, and where thieves do not break in and steal. For where your treasure is, there your heart will be also.

Luke 12:15
Then [Jesus] said to them, "Watch out! Be on your guard against all kinds of greed; a man's life does not consist in the abundance of his possessions."

Life Changers

- Talk to your parents or to a financial planner from your church before you sign any kind of financial agreement.
- For more comprehensive insight into the confusing world of money, finance, and personal budgeting, read *Master Your Money* by Ron Blue.

Five-Finger Discount

The door flies open. Cindi and Patty burst into the room laughing and gasping for breath. Marie looks up from the magazine she's reading.

"Quick!" motions Cindi. "Grab your pillow and come with us."

"What's up?" Marie wants to know.

"Just hurry."

Marie grabs her pillow and follows her friends down the stairs to the third floor vending machine area. Cindi stands guard in the hallway, while Patty goes over to a snack machine and sticks her long, skinny arm up into the bin. Marie hears a clicking noise and then watches in amazement as Patty retrieves a "complimentary" candy bar.

"How'd, uh . . . I mean, where . . . um, how'd you do that?" she sputters.

Patty smiles. "My older brother showed me how to do it on certain vending machines. Isn't it great? In ten minutes we can get enough junk food to last us for a month!"

Marie is suddenly very nervous. "Yeah, but what if you get caught?"

Patty makes a face. "How? How are we going to get caught? Cindi's standing watch over there. Here, give me the pillow."

In a matter of minutes, Patty has retrieved no less than three dozen assorted treats and stuffed them inside the pillowcase. Suddenly, Cindi bolts into the room. "Somebody's coming!"

Cindi is clearly nervous. Marie is scared to death.

"I knew this was a bad idea. I should have never come with y'all!" she blurts.

"Just act normal!" Patty snaps as the footsteps in the hallway get closer.

Thought Joggers

- Why are so many people so quick to try to take advantage of others?
- How much stealing or pilfering would go on in the world if everyone copied *your* standards and *your* behavior?
- Assuming you have had something stolen from you, can you remember how you felt?
- How do you typically respond when faced with the situation of "getting (through unethical or sinful means) something for nothing"?
- What is Marie's best course of action?

Eye-Openers

Consider two biblical principles that relate to the subject above:

Luke 6:31
Do to others as you would have them do to you.

In other words: God's people are to be governed by the "Golden Rule."

Romans 13:9–10
The commandments, "Do not commit adultery," "Do not murder," "Do not steal," "Do not covet," and whatever other commandment there may be, are summed up in this one rule: "Love your neighbor as yourself." Love does no harm to its neighbor. Therefore love is the fulfillment of the law.

In other words: The Golden Rule can be summarized in one word: "Love!"

Life Changers

- Ask God for the strength of character to walk away from bad situations (regardless of how your friends might respond).
- Ask a close Christian friend to "get in your face" the next time you start to make a bad choice. Such accountability in friendships can often be the main factor in keeping us from unwise, sinful actions.
- Read the story of Joshua and Caleb and how they bravely stood alone against a whole nation of people who were insistent on doing the wrong thing (Numbers 13–14).

"Free" Cable

Bob and Marj Freace have applied the same rule to each of their five kids: Within three months after you graduate from high school, you're expected to move out and move on. You can go to college or go to work, but if you hang around the house, you start paying rent. Eighteen-year-old Lee decided he'd move into an apartment with Tom, a high school buddy, and begin saving money for college.

After a week of searching, he and Tom found the perfect place—a one-bedroom apartment with a built-in washer and dryer. After paying numerous deposits and connection fees, the guys discovered something surprising the day they moved in. Though they had signed up for basic cable service only, they were somehow getting two of the premium pay channels that show first-run movies.

Lee started to pick up the phone to call the cable company. "I told them we didn't want those channels. Great! That's all we need—a huge cable bill on top of everything else."

Tom grabbed the phone away from Lee. "No, man, hold up! Don't call yet. Maybe they made a mistake. Let's wait and see what our first bill looks like. If they end up charging us for those channels, we'll just go in and complain. We'll tell them we never ordered the expanded service, and we don't want it. But we'll still end up getting a month's worth of free movies."

"And what if they don't bill us for those channels?"

"Well, then, we're set. We get HBO and Cinemax at no charge!"

Lee isn't sure what to think of Tom's plan, but just then he notices one of his favorite movies about to begin. The guys grab some soft drinks out of the refrigerator and sit down to watch.

Thought Joggers

- Why is it that most people facing a moral dilemma ask themselves, What can I get away with? rather than, What is the right thing to do?
- What do you think about the Freaces' policy of "forcing" their children to move out? Why?
- What is the difference between taking something from somebody and taking advantage of somebody?
- Which word would you use to describe Tom's plan: shrewd, dishonest, unethical, sneaky, ingenious, or foolproof? Why?
- What would you do in Lee's situation? Why?

Eye-Openers

Consider these principles from Proverbs that relate to the story above:

Proverbs 16:8
Better a little with righteousness
than much gain with injustice.

In other words: It's better to live honestly even if that means doing without.

Proverbs 28:6
Better a poor man whose walk is blameless
than a rich man whose ways are perverse.

In other words: Having character is far more valuable than having things.

Proverbs 20:17
Food gained by fraud tastes sweet to a man,
but he ends up with a mouth full of gravel.

In other words: Dishonest gain causes long-term pain.

Life Changers

- Ask God to help you get in the habit of viewing situations in terms of "what is right and what is wrong?" rather than "what can I get away with here?"
- Examine your own life for areas of compromise—for instances of trying to take advantage or instances of trying to "sneak one past" someone else.

Moving Out

Ever since he can remember, Kenneth has been fascinated with fixing things. He has repaired everything from toasters to lawn mowers to a policeman's broken-down motorcycle. But his *specialty* is cars. Give Kenneth a well-equipped toolbox and put him in front of a raised hood, and Kenneth feels like he's died and gone to heaven.

At the beginning of his senior year Kenneth met Mr. Gugliuzza, the manager of the local GMC dealership. One thing led to another and—to make a long story short—Kenneth has been offered a mechanic's position beginning in June after he graduates.

Kenneth's dad thinks this is a great opportunity for Kenneth to get some experience and begin saving some money. By living at home he can probably sack away $500 a month. But Kenneth has other ideas. He wants to move in with a couple of friends who are older and who have an apartment. He feels like it is time that he experiences life on his own.

The problem is that these older friends stay out late, sleep late, and each has been fired at least once. They're nice guys, but they aren't very disciplined. They aren't responsible, either.

Kenneth's dad worries that their bad habits will rub off on Kenneth and possibly cost him his job. He also is afraid that Kenneth's salary will be consumed by rent and utility bills. Kenneth gets angry every time his dad brings up the subject.

Thought Joggers

- What would be the perfect job for you?
- What are the pros and cons of Kenneth's moving out versus his living at home?
- What makes it hard for you to live at home? What do you like about living at home?
- Why do you think Kenneth gets angry when his dad brings up the subject?
- What would you likely do in this situation?

Eye-Openers

Consider the following biblical passages as they relate to wisdom for Kenneth (and for those in similar situations):

Proverbs 10:4
Lazy hands make a man poor,
   but diligent hands bring wealth.

Proverbs 14:23
All hard work brings a profit,
   but mere talk leads only to poverty.

Proverbs 19:15
Laziness brings on deep sleep,
   and the shiftless man goes hungry.

In other words: God expects hard work.

Proverbs 13:1
A wise son heeds his father's instruction,
   but a mocker does not listen to rebuke.

Proverbs 13:13
He who scorns instruction will pay for it,
but he who respects a command is rewarded.

Proverbs 16:20
Whoever gives heed to instruction prospers,
and blessed is he who trusts in the LORD.

Proverbs 19:20
Listen to advice and accept instruction,
and in the end you will be wise.

In other words: God expects us to pay attention to wise counsel.

1 Corinthians 15:33
Do not be misled: "Bad company corrupts good character."

In other words: God expects us to choose friends wisely.

Life Changers

- Sit down with a parent or another adult whom you respect and trust and come up with a monthly budget. Try to determine exactly what it costs to live on your own in your city.
- Talk to an older friend or sibling about what it's like to live away from home. (Don't merely ask questions about the positive aspects of living on one's own—also discuss the negatives of moving out.)
- Ask your parents about their first experiences with living away from home as well as their first jobs.

Blowing the Whistle on a Coworker

Sonya has a full-time job at Simone, a popular clothing store in the mall. She's been working there since she was a junior in high school. Now that she's graduated (and since she's been an excellent employee), there has been talk that Sonya may soon be promoted to assistant manager.

Tonight as Sonya was closing, she observed Mrs. Rodham, an older woman and the only other employee on duty at the time, fold a pair of $40 shorts and slip them into her purse.

Maybe she paid for them when I wasn't looking, Sonya thought, so she said nothing. But after Mrs. Rodham left, Sonya checked the cash register receipts. She found no record of any shorts of that style being sold all day long.

As Sonya drove home, she wondered what to do. *Mrs. Rodham is old enough to be my mom! I feel weird saying anything to her. And besides, what if there's an explanation I haven't considered? . . . But then again, what if she just flat out stole those shorts? If I don't say anything, the store loses money, and maybe I get in trouble for not keeping up with the inventory!*

Sonya tossed and turned for two hours before she finally drifted off to sleep.

Thought Joggers

- What are the consequences to both parties if Sonya blows the whistle on Mrs. Rodham?

- Should Sonya confront Mrs. Rodham directly? If so, how could she do so in a nonjudgmental way?
- What other options does Sonya have?
- What would you tell Sonya to do if she asked for your advice?
- What do you think you would actually do in a similar situation?

Eye-Openers

The Bible specifies that in our dealings with other people, we must always be "speaking the truth in love" (Eph. 4:15) no matter what the consequences. Consider how the following individuals obeyed God and told the truth even in some very touchy situations:

- Nathan, when confronting King David about his adultery (2 Sam. 12:1–14)
- Jeremiah, when rebuking the nation of Judah for their sin (Jer. 26)
- Jesus, when discussing the scribes and Pharisees (Matt. 23)
- Peter and John, before the religious leaders of Israel (Acts 4:1–20)

Life Changers

- Share the above scenario with your parents. Ask them what they would do in that situation.
- In your everyday conversation, seek to avoid "loaded language" (i.e., words, phrases, tones of

voice, or facial expressions that usually cause other people to become defensive and angry). Try to be neutral and nonjudgmental, especially when you confront someone else over an issue of behavior. Get in the habit of evaluating your speech on the basis of Ephesians 4:15. Ask, Am I being truthful? and, Am I being loving?

Friendly Discounts

After graduation in mid-May three of Randy's best friends enrolled at a nearby community college, and another joined the Marines. Not Randy. He used his considerable knowledge of cars to land a job as an assistant manager-in-training at a new auto parts store in town.

It's a great job for someone right out of high school—salary plus insurance benefits (after six months). And then there is the employee discount on merchandise . . . Randy is counting on that perk to save him some big money when he gets ready to overhaul his '71 Mustang.

Last week a couple of old friends from high school came to the store to see Randy. They were obviously impressed with the shiny new store and with Randy's position. "Do you realize how lucky you are to get a job like this?" they asked. "We're cooking burgers for minimum wage, and you're eighteen and already starting your career!"

Randy could hardly contain his pride. He felt important—so much so that when one of the guys mentioned the need for some spark plugs, Randy walked with him over to aisle four. "Here," he said, handing his surprised friend a box of Champions.

"What's this? You mean I can *have* these—for free?"

"Yeah, just don't go telling everybody where you got them."

"Randy! Man, thanks. You're awesome!"

Randy's smile lit up the room. "Hey, I've got to look out for my friends, right?"

Thought Joggers

- What do you think prompted this display of generosity on Randy's part?
- How commonly do you think store clerks and managers of retail stores offer similar "discounts" to their friends and/or relatives?
- Since Randy was just trying to be nice, since his action might actually increase future business, and since the company will probably never miss a few spark plugs, why was his action wrong?
- What are the possible consequences of Randy's action?
- How would you feel if friends tried to pressure you into cutting them a questionable deal? How do you think you might respond?

Eye-Openers

Consider the integrity and honesty displayed by Joseph in Genesis 39 when he refused to take advantage of his "boss":

From the time he [Potiphar, Joseph's master] put him [Joseph] in charge of his household and of all that he owned, the LORD blessed the household of the Egyptian because of Joseph. The blessing of the LORD was on everything Potiphar had, both in the house and in the field. So he left in Joseph's care everything he had; with

Joseph in charge, he did not concern himself with anything except the food he ate.

Now Joseph was well-built and handsome, and after a while his master's wife took notice of Joseph and said, "Come to bed with me!"

But he refused. "With me in charge," he told her, "my master does not concern himself with anything in the house; everything he owns he has entrusted to my care. No one is greater in this house than I am. My master has withheld nothing from me except you, because you are his wife. How then could I do such a wicked thing and sin against God?"

Life Changers

- Get with a Christian friend and list the most difficult temptations you face on the job.
- Pray together for the strength to live for Christ while you are working.
- To insure that you don't break any company rules, ask your employer to provide you with an employee policy manual (or go back and read the one you already have).

Pulling Strings

"Hey, Mom, guess what?"

"What?"

"Some guy is coming to church next week to interview graduating seniors for summer jobs at this Christian camp."

"Oh, and what camp is that?"

"It's called Clear Springs Conference Center."

"Really? Clear Springs? I think your dad went to school with the man who's the director there."

"He did?"

"Yeah, they played baseball together."

"I guess it's a small world, huh?"

"I guess it is. So, Gene, what kind of job are you thinking you'd like to apply for?"

"I'm not sure. I'm pretty good with horses, so I could be a stable hand. Or there's always the kitchen staff or the work crew. But I'm not holding my breath. They're only going to hire about thirty seniors. And I heard they get about 300 applicants."

"What about being a cabin counselor?"

"You have to be a college student to be a counselor."

"Oh, I see. Well, your dad will be excited to hear all about it."

At supper that night, Gene mentions his desire to go to Clear Springs. His dad gets so excited he can barely contain himself.

"Gene, that's great! That would be the experience of a lifetime. You know, the director there and I are old friends. We played college ball together. I can give John a call tomorrow and put in a good word for you."

Gene isn't sure what to say. It sounds like his dad could pull a few strings and get him a position. At the same time, Gene would like to try to get the job on his own.

Thought Joggers

- What advantages do you have over others because of family ties or friendship connections?
- What, if anything, is wrong with pulling strings or having them pulled for you?
- Put yourself in Gene's shoes. Which would be worse: to get the job (but only because your dad made a phone call), or to not get the job because someone else beat you out?
- How important is it for you to make your own way in the world?
- What, in your opinion, should Gene do?

Eye-Openers

Jeremiah 9:23–24 stresses our need to trust in the Lord, not in our own abilities or human advantages:

This is what the LORD says: "Let not the wise man boast of his wisdom or the strong man boast of his strength or the rich man boast of his riches, but let him who boasts boast about this: that he understands and knows me, that I am the LORD, who exercises kindness, justice and righteousness on earth, for in these I delight," declares the LORD.

Life Changers

- Ask God for the courage to trust in him *alone* as you prepare for life after high school.
- Part of growing up is learning to stand on your own. If you have parents who are trying to program or run your life, gently explain to them that while you value their advice, you want to learn to make your own decisions. Thank them for their willingness to help, but share with them your desire for more independence.

Questionable Employment

Jeff knew he might have problems getting a job in a small college town, but he never expected *this* degree of difficulty. There's not one job opening on campus, and Jeff can't even find work at a fast-food restaurant!

With a checking account balance of $3.19, Jeff is getting more than a little nervous. So he decides to head over to the Student Center to look one more time at the SGA Job Board. Just as he arrives to scan the few remaining notices, a bearded man walks up.

"Looking for a job?" the stranger inquires.

"Yeah," Jeff mumbles. "I've been hunting for three weeks straight. I can't believe there's so little work in this town! Heck, at this point, I'd be willing to *baby-sit*—and I don't even know how to change a diaper!"

The man smiles broadly. "Well, I don't have any baby-sitting openings, but I *am* looking for a clerk for my store. This just might be your lucky day."

"What kind of store do you have?"

"Have you heard of Bradley's Beer Barn?"

"Uh, yeah."

"Well, I'm Bradley. And I need a new clerk to operate the drive-thru window on Friday and Saturday nights. If you worked out, I'd pay you $6 an hour."

Jeff's head is spinning with all kinds of contrasting thoughts. *Six bucks an hour. That's more than minimum wage! . . . But what would my parents say if they knew that I took a job selling beer? But, on the other hand, look at my*

checking account. It's not like I'd be drinking the beer myself.
And if I didn't sell it, someone else would. Then again, what
would my Christian friends say if they saw me sitting in the
drive-thru window of the Beer Barn?

Jeff's thoughts are interrupted. "Well, whaddya say?
I gotta find somebody quick. If you don't want the job,
I'm sure I can find someone who does."

Jeff suddenly feels panicky, desperate, and confused.

Thought Joggers

- Would it be wrong for Jeff to take a job selling beer at Bradley's Beer Barn? Why or why not?
- What do you think about Jeff's reasoning?
- How do you feel about other jobs where Christians must deal with alcohol—waiters or waitresses who serve it, stockers who put it on the shelves, delivery personnel who transport it? Are any of these jobs inappropriate? Why or why not?
- How do you think *you* might respond in a situation like the one just described?
- What is it about stressful situations that cause us to rationalize more than usual?

Eye-Openers

Consider these Bible passages and how each might apply to Jeff's situation:

Proverbs 20:1
Wine is a mocker and beer a brawler;
  whoever is led astray by them is not wise.

What does this passage say about the potential dangers of alcohol?

What are some ways you have seen this truth come to pass in real life?

Philippians 1:9–10
And this is my prayer: that your love may abound more and more in knowledge and depth of insight, so that you may be able to discern what is best and may be pure and blameless until the day of Christ.

What is discernment and why is it important?

Where could Jeff gain insight and discernment for making a tough decision?

Life Changers

- If you are job hunting, stop and list those jobs that would violate your convictions or would cause you to compromise your faith.
- Find an older, wiser Christian friend who can act as a sounding board for you when you are struggling through tough decisions.

The Brazen Boss

How in the world did a sweet Christian girl like Amy end up in the sack with her boss? Here's her shocking story.

Amy took a summer job doing an internship with Mitch Davidson, a successful architect who attends her church. A triathlete in his mid-thirties, Mitch is handsome with an engaging personality. He also has a great sense of humor.

At the beginning of the summer, Amy mostly answered the phone, set up appointments, and ran errands. But in July Mitch began asking Amy to ride with him to look at certain building projects. He listened intently whenever she talked about her dream of studying architecture in college. The two talked for hours about their lives, about Mitch's failed marriage, even about God and faith. Often they ate lunch together. And once, Mitch even took Amy with him on a one day trip by chartered jet to talk to a client in Chicago.

Yesterday, after going out to look at a renovation project in town, Mitch said, "Hey, Amy, I just got an idea. Last night after work I stopped at the grocery store and bought all the ingredients for this shrimp and angel hair pasta dish I had once at a restaurant in New Orleans. It's kind of depressing to think of going home tonight and cooking for one. Whaddya say we swing by my place and eat lunch there?"

"Sure!" Amy replied, flattered to get to spend time with such a sweet guy.

Mitch's place was what Amy expected—like something out of *Architectural Digest*. But what happened once they got there was most unexpected. Somehow as they were preparing lunch, laughing, and talking in the kitchen, they ended up looking deeply into each other's eyes. They started kissing. Amy felt overwhelmed and out of control. The next thing she knew they were in bed together.

Thought Joggers

- How could something like this have happened to two Christians?
- What could (and should) Amy and Mitch have done to have guarded against this kind of involvement?
- After hearing this story, what do you think about Mitch?
- What is your opinion of Amy?
- How can you guard yourself against inappropriate premarital sexual/physical involvement?

Eye-Openers

First Thessalonians 4:1–8 stresses the divine requirement that we be sexually pure:

Finally, brothers, we instructed you how to live in order to please God, as in fact you are living. Now we ask you and urge you in the Lord Jesus to do this more and more. For you know what instructions we gave you by the authority of the Lord Jesus.

It is God's will that you should be sanctified: that you should avoid sexual immorality; that each of you should learn to control his own body in a way that is holy and honorable, not in passionate lust like the heathen, who do not know God; and that in this matter no one should wrong his brother or take advantage of him. The Lord will punish men for all such sins, as we have already told you and warned you. For God did not call us to be impure, but to live a holy life. Therefore, he who rejects this instruction does not reject man but God, who gives you his Holy Spirit.

Other passages warn us to be alert and careful so that we don't end up in places we'd rather not be:

1 Thessalonians 5:6
So then, let us not be like others, who are asleep, but let us be alert and self-controlled.

1 Peter 1:13
Therefore, prepare your minds for action; be self-controlled; set your hope fully on the grace to be given you when Jesus Christ is revealed.

1 Peter 4:7
The end of all things is near. Therefore be clear minded and self-controlled so that you can pray.

Life Changers
- Ask God for the wisdom to notice when you start drifting towards trouble and for the strength to say no to sinful desires.
- Make sure you have a close Christian friend (who

is courageous and truthful) who always knows what is happening in your life. He or she may be all that is standing in the way of you and a messed-up life!

- Memorize one of the passages above. Why is Scripture memory valuable? (See Psalm 119:11.)

The "Perks" at Work

When Brad graduated from high school, he didn't feel ready for college. So he found a job working for a small janitorial service that cleans office buildings after hours. He likes his job because he can sleep in the mornings and because he is able to work unsupervised. Plus, with only one building to clean every night, he never feels rushed. Whether he does the work in three hours or five hours, he is paid the same.

One night about a month ago, Brad overheard a conversation between two secretaries who were working late. Apparently the insurance agent they worked for had installed some sort of toll-free phone line.

Over the next few days, Brad snooped around a little bit and confirmed his suspicions. Driving home one night soon after that, he hit on a plan: *Why not arrange for all my friends from camp to call me long distance on that toll-free line late on certain evenings? The building will be empty, the call is already paid for, we'll only talk for a few minutes, and then I'll hurry and finish my cleaning. No one will be hurt and no one will ever know.*

The next week Brad implemented his idea. For several weeks he enjoyed catching up with his friends around the country. But last night, just as Brad finished talking with Andrew, a friend from the Pacific Northwest, his boss stepped into the darkened office.

"Alright, Brad, we need to have a little talk—now!"

Thought Joggers

- How does supervision change the habits of employees? Why is this so?
- Brad is not the kind of guy who would think of stealing money or taking property. What do you think caused him to cook up a scheme for free phone calls?
- Is Brad's behavior really *wrong*? Why or why not?
- What are some of the ways your friends take advantage of their employers?
- What are the possible consequences for Brad?

Eye-Openers

The words found in Ephesians 6:5–8 were originally written to slaves, but the principles they convey apply more broadly to all employees. Consider the wisdom found in these verses:

> Slaves, obey your earthly masters with respect and fear, and with sincerity of heart, just as you would obey Christ. Obey them not only to win their favor when their eye is on you, but like slaves of Christ, doing the will of God from your heart. Serve wholeheartedly, as if you were serving the Lord, not men, because you know that the Lord will reward everyone for whatever good he does, whether he is slave or free.

Life Changers

- Try to get into the habit of working at your job as though Christ were standing there supervising you. (He *is*, you know!)

- If you have stolen or "borrowed" something from an employer, make restitution. Explain to your boss your actions, ask for forgiveness and a second chance, and vow to pay what you owe. This will be one of the most difficult experiences of your life, but it will do wonders for your conscience, and it will deter future improprieties.

Abortion

Vanessa and Rebecca have known each other since middle school, but during high school—through shared experiences in class, in theater productions, and in youth group—the girls have become the very best of friends. They have often talked—especially during their senior year—about moving to New York together and pursuing acting careers.

Since graduation, however, Rebecca has been spending all her time with her new boyfriend. She didn't even bother to try out for a summer production of *Oklahoma*. (Odd, since that particular musical is Rebecca's favorite!) Anyway, enough background . . . here's the story.

Last night after getting home from rehearsal, Vanessa received a call from Rebecca. She was obviously upset.

"Hey, what's the matter?"

"Oh, Vanessa. I'm so glad you're there! I'm in trouble. I'm in *big* trouble."

"What?"

"I don't know how to say this," she sobbed. "But, um, I uh, I'm . . . pregnant!"

"Rebecca, what?! Are you kidding me?"

"Oh, Vanessa, I wish I were kidding. I'm so scared! This is like a bad dream. My parents just *can't* find out. They would be destroyed."

Vanessa feels sick to her stomach. There's a long uncomfortable silence while she tries to think of what to say. Finally Rebecca sniffs, "I guess I can always get an abortion."

"Rebecca, what are you saying? You can't do that!"

"What other options do I have?"

With her best friend talking about pregnancy and abortion, Vanessa feels like *she's* the one in a bad dream!

Thought Joggers

- What difficulties would be involved in having a baby and then putting it up for adoption?
- What difficulties are involved in "terminating a pregnancy"?
- Besides avoiding public embarrassment, what are the reasons someone would have an abortion?
- Realistically, what can you do to help your friends stay out of situations like the one above?
- What would you tell Rebecca?
- What would you advise Vanessa to do?
- Should Vanessa tell Rebecca's parents? Why or why not?

Eye-Openers

Consider two Bible passages that depict the humanity and precious value of each unborn child:

Psalm 139:13–16

For you created my inmost being;
> you knit me together in my mother's womb.

I praise you because I am fearfully and wonderfully made;
> your works are wonderful,
> I know that full well.

My frame was not hidden from you
> when I was made in the secret place.
When I was woven together in the depths of the earth,
> your eyes saw my unformed body.
All the days ordained for me
> were written in your book
> before one of them came to be.

Luke 1:41–44
When Elizabeth heard Mary's greeting, the baby leaped in her womb, and Elizabeth was filled with the Holy Spirit. In a loud voice she exclaimed: "Blessed are you among women, and blessed is the child you will bear! But why am I so favored, that the mother of my Lord should come to me? As soon as the sound of your greeting reached my ears, the baby in my womb leaped for joy."

Life Changers

- Abortion is an issue that is not going to go away. Make sure you know where you stand on this important issue. Ask your pastor or youth leader to recommend a good book or article on the subject.
- Pray for the strength to remain sexually pure from now until the time you marry.
- Share the scenario above with your parents and/or your youth leader. Get their advice as to whether it is appropriate to keep a secret like the one Rebecca asked Vanessa to keep.

Lust Control

Taylor knew college life would feature a lot of pretty girls, but he had no idea that being in the "Land of Babes" would turn his two best Christian friends into "out-of-control" girl-watchers.

During the waning days of summer (when school was just beginning), their big thing was, "Hey, Taylor, let's go check out the girls on the sundeck." When the weather turned cool it was, "You gotta come with us to the intramural complex. There's a coed aerobics class at three today, and you can't believe how gorgeous some of the girls there are."

Going to and from the cafeteria, or to and from class, or to and from *anywhere*, these guys constantly have their radar up, scanning the campus for attractive females. They're pretty obvious. In fact, today one of the guys almost gave himself whiplash looking back at one of the school cheerleaders after she had passed. Taylor had seen enough.

"Do you realize how stupid you look when you do that?"

"Do what?"

"Practically break your neck staring at girls' bodies."

"Oh, like you don't look!"

"Hey, I'm not the one who goes to the pool or to the intramural center every day and stands there drooling like some sort of deprived sex fiend!"

"Sheesh, what's with you?"

"What's with *you!* You just embarrass yourself—and me—when you act so immature. It's like you've never seen a girl before."

"Man, you're a jerk! Where do you get off lecturing me about girl-watching? Like you don't ever do it!"

Taylor watches his angry friend walk away in a huff. *Maybe I was kind of harsh,* he reasons to himself. *But I have enough trouble keeping my thoughts pure without having my best friends talk about girls and their bodies all the time!*

Thought Joggers

- Guys seem to "girl-watch" more than girls "guy-watch." Why do you think this is so?
- How might Taylor have handled his situation differently?
- Do you think it is really possible to change mental habits and clean up your thought life? Why or why not?
- Why do you think some guys struggle more than others with the temptation to lust?

Eye-Openers

Here are some Bible principles and passages that can help in situations like the one Taylor is facing:

1 Corinthians 10:13

No temptation has seized you except what is common to man. And God is faithful; he will not let you be tempted beyond what you can bear. But when you are tempted, he will also provide a way out so that you can stand up under it.

In other words: Temptation, even the temptation to lust, is resistible.

2 Corinthians 10:5
We demolish arguments and every pretension that sets itself up against the knowledge of God, and we take captive every thought to make it obedient to Christ.

In other words: To win the battle against lust, we must carefully monitor our thoughts.

Hebrews 12:2
Let us fix our eyes on Jesus, the author and perfecter of our faith, who for the joy set before him endured the cross, scorning its shame, and sat down at the right hand of the throne of God.

In other words: To win the battle against lust, we must consciously fill our minds with thoughts of Christ and his kingdom.

Life Changers

- (Guys) Ask your dad or your pastor how he fights the battle against lust.
- (Girls) Ask your dad or your pastor to give you a guy's perspective on lust and sexual temptation.
- Share this book with a friend when you finish it. (Or better yet, encourage every student in your high school to buy this book!)

Porno Plague

Josh never imagined when he agreed to move in with Gary that he would also be sharing living quarters with numerous naked women. Lest you misunderstand, here's the situation: In the last couple of weeks, Gary has plastered the walls of their room with all sorts of erotic posters and foldouts. No matter what direction Josh looks, he ends up staring at a beautiful body, or two or three or more! He finds it hard to sleep, to study, to brush his teeth, to do *anything* in the room without thinking lustful thoughts.

As a red-blooded male with normal sexual urges and as a Christian who wants to live a pure life, Josh is absolutely going crazy inside. Here's how he puts it: "I can't keep living like this. Whenever I'm in the room, I feel completely powerless to keep from looking at those pictures. I'm telling you, it's addicting! Even when I leave the room, I can't get those images out of my head. Then I feel like a major hypocrite. I'm supposed to focus on godly things. And I should *want* to turn away from those kinds of thoughts. And I guess deep down inside, I *do* want to turn away. But if I'm honest, part of me really enjoys looking at that stuff. What *really* scares me is that I know Gary has some porno tapes in his desk. My big temptation now is that I'm fighting the urge to watch those on our VCR when Gary's not in the room."

Thought Joggers

- (For guys) What is it about pornography that makes it so enticing and, often, so addicting?
- Should pornography be banned? Why or why not?
- What, if anything, could Josh say to Gary to try to change the situation?
- Some people argue that God made *both* the human body *and* the act of sex; therefore, the reasoning goes, nudity is a beautiful, natural thing. What's wrong with this argument?
- What are the ramifications if Josh says nothing and does nothing about his living situation?
- What would you tell Josh to do?

Eye-Openers

Consider these Bible passages and principles which provide insight for the situation in which Josh finds himself:

Matthew 5:27–28

You have heard that it was said, "Do not commit adultery." But I tell you that anyone who looks at a woman lustfully has already committed adultery with her in his heart.

In other words: Thinking impure thoughts is just as wrong in the sight of God as doing impure acts.

Philippians 4:8

Finally, brothers, whatever is true, whatever is noble, whatever is right, whatever is pure, whatever is lovely, whatever is admirable—if anything is excellent or praiseworthy—think about such things.

In other words: Filling your mind with pure thoughts is one way to avoid thinking impure thoughts.

Job 31:1
I made a covenant with my eyes
   not to look lustfully at a girl.

In other words: A pure thought life requires a firm commitment.

Life Changers

- If you are a female, carefully consider how you dress and talk and act. Don't add to the sexual temptations that your boyfriend and/or male friends are already experiencing.
- If you are a male, please understand that lust is an insatiable enemy that can literally consume and wreck your life. Our nation's prisons are filled with convicted sex offenders who began by "innocently" peeking at a steamy video or magazine. Be *extremely* careful about the kinds of images you expose your eyes to!
- Discuss with your Christian friends what types of movies, videos, books, and magazines are acceptable, and what types are unacceptable.

Shack Attack!

Sarah had heard stories—*wild* stories—about college life, but she still wasn't prepared for what she found when she arrived on campus this fall. Rivers of alcohol, unending parties, incredibly creative cheating techniques. But perhaps the thing that has shocked Sarah most is the major amount of "shacking" that goes on.

"Shacking" is the name Tech students give to the practice of staying the night in your date's room or sweetheart's apartment. Shacking doesn't *automatically* equal sexual involvement, but in many cases that's what ends up happening.

Friday night Sarah and two other girlfriends ended up at the apartment of some older guys. They cooked out. They all watched a video. No big romantic thing except maybe for Christy and Mike. (They definitely seemed to be hitting it off nicely.) The group talked and laughed. They played cards. Then it was late (or early, depending on your point of view). At last everyone started yawning.

"Why don't you guys just crash here?"

Before Sarah could open her mouth, Christy said, "Yeah, that'll be great."

Sarah is freaking out! What is she going to do? She knows people shack all the time. But what will other people think if they see her coming out of the guys' apartment in the morning—or not returning to the dorm until tomorrow? What would her mom say if she found out? She can't just leave—Christy is her ride home. And Christy suddenly looks like she's had Mike surgically attached to her body! Should she call someone back at the dorm? If she does, will people think she's weird?

Sarah excuses herself to the bathroom. She sits on the edge of the tub and suddenly feels as though she's going to throw up.

Thought Joggers

- If there is no sex involved, what's wrong with shacking?
- What, if anything, can one person do to change the attitudes or the actions of a big group?
- How might your reputation be affected by shacking?
- What are Sarah's best options?
- What would you do if you were Sarah?

Eye-Openers

Consider these principles that relate to the scenario above:

Proverbs 22:1
A good name is more desirable than great riches;
to be esteemed is better than silver or gold.

In other words: Our reputation as believers is very important.

1 Peter 1:13–15
Therefore, prepare your minds for action; be self-controlled; set your hope fully on the grace to be given you when Jesus Christ is revealed. As obedient children, do not conform to the evil desires you had when you lived in ignorance. But just as he who called you is holy, so be holy in all you do.

In other words: A holy lifestyle should be our goal in life.

1 Peter 2:11–12
Dear friends, I urge you, as aliens and strangers in the world, to abstain from sinful desires, which war against your soul. Live such good lives among the pagans that, though they accuse you of doing wrong, they may see your good deeds and glorify God on the day he visits us.

In other words: When we live pure lives, others are affected.

Life Changers

- To find out more about the kinds of compromising situations you will encounter at college, interview a Christian college student or two. Knowing what to expect can help you prepare.
- Make up a prayer list and distribute it to Christian friends and family members. Ask them to pray daily for you while you are away at school.

Road Trip

Bret, Alyson, and a handful of friends are finishing up a large "Sweep the Kitchen" pizza at Louie's on Thursday night when the conversation shifts to weekend plans.

"I've got to work Saturday," moans Hank.

"Yeah, well, *I* need to study," says Holly. "I've got two tests on Tuesday."

Alyson pipes up. "I probably *should* stick around and study. But I told my mom I'd come home for the weekend. What about you, Bret?"

Bret grabs the last piece of pizza. "I don't have any *definite* plans . . . But I was sort of thinking about heading down to the beach."

"The beach?" Holly almost chokes. "That's a ten-hour drive!"

Bret smiles. "Only eight and a half if *I'm* driving. In fact, if we left within the next hour, we could get there in time to see the sunrise."

Todd's ears perk up. "Do I smell a road trip?"

The friends begin to look around at each other as if to say, "Well?"

Bret continues his sales pitch. "Before you say no, I should tell you all that I saw the weather forecast for tomorrow: Clear, sunny, with a high of eighty-five."

"I'm there!" Todd almost yells. "How many opportunities do we get to do things like this? We'll come back Sunday afternoon. How about it, everybody?"

It's apparent that wills are weakening all around the table.

Hank is wondering what excuse he can give his boss.

Holly is rationalizing about the seventeen hours of intense "study time" she'll have in the car to and from the beach.

Alyson is trying to come up with a sneaky way to tell her mom she won't be coming home after all. "I'll have to make up something good—I'm staying to look after a sick friend, or maybe that I'm going on a church retreat. I can't just tell her I went to the beach!"

Bret is pleased by the positive response of the group. "Everybody go grab your stuff and meet back here in forty-five minutes!"

Thought Joggers

- What makes spontaneous, impulsive road trips so much fun?
- In what ways are spontaneous, impulsive road trips not a good idea?
- What criteria do you use to make spur-of-the-moment decisions?
- What are the possible consequences for people who let their peers (or feelings or desires) make all their decisions?
- What would be the wisest course of action for each of the characters in the above story?

Eye-Openers

If you are easily swayed by friends into making unwise choices, consider these biblical passages and principles:

Proverbs 25:28
Like a city whose walls are broken down
is a man who lacks self-control.

In other words: A life without rules or boundaries leads to disaster.

Genesis 13:7–12:
And quarreling arose between Abram's herdsmen and the herdsmen of Lot. The Canaanites and Perizzites were also living in the land at that time.

So Abram said to Lot, "Let's not have any quarreling between you and me, or between your herdsmen and mine, for we are brothers. Is not the whole land before you? Let's part company. If you go to the left, I'll go to the right; if you go to the right, I'll go to the left."

Lot looked up and saw that the whole plain of the Jordan was well watered, like the garden of the LORD, like the land of Egypt, toward Zoar. (This was before the LORD destroyed Sodom and Gomorrah.) So Lot chose for himself the whole plain of the Jordan and set out toward the east. The two men parted company: Abram lived in the land of Canaan, while Lot lived among the cities of the plain and pitched his tents near Sodom. (Note: The text goes on to report the terrible effects that living near Sodom had on Lot and his family.)

In other words: Decisions that are made without first carefully considering all the facts often produce nothing but pain and regret.

Life Changers

- A wise individual once said, "Get in the habit of saying no to at least one thing every day." This person recognized the value of self-control and the importance of not trying to do anything and everything in life.
- Ask an adult you respect to tell you how he or she makes wise decisions.

Barhopping?

This afternoon Jim is faced with what is becoming a recurring dilemma: Should he go out with his friends tonight? It doesn't sound like a big deal until you realize that Jim's friends like to frequent several different bars so they can meet girls, listen to music, and shoot pool.

"On the one hand," Jim reasons, "I don't drink, so it's not like I'm going out with all these thoughts of getting smashed. In fact, most of the time I end up being the designated driver for my friends who are in no condition to drive themselves home. I sometimes wonder what might happen to them if I didn't go! Plus, part of me feels like maybe if people see me there with a Coke in my hand, and I'm laughing and having a good time, maybe they'll realize it's possible to have fun without drinking.

"On the other hand," Jim continues, "some of my Christian friends think I'm compromising my faith by going to bars. They say it looks bad, that people will assume I am drinking, and that I just shouldn't be in places like that. I'll admit, it's not the greatest atmosphere in the world, but I really do care about my friends, and I like being with them.

"Of course if my parents knew I was even going within 100 feet of a bar, they'd go ballistic!"

Thought Joggers

- What do you think about Jim's reasoning?

- Jim has no desire to drink, so that's not really an issue. But what other issues or concerns are raised by his behavior?
- In your opinion, is it wrong to go into a bar? What about a restaurant that serves alcohol? What about a grocery store that sells alcohol? How did you arrive at these convictions and why? What is the basis for your feelings?
- Are there ever situations in which it would be appropriate or acceptable for a Christian to frequent a "questionable" establishment (like a bar)?
- How can we figure out what our real motives are in a situation like the one above?
- What would you advise Jim to do if he came to you for advice?

Eye-Openers

Consider two biblical examples that speak to Jim's situation:

Matthew 9:9–13

As Jesus went on from there, he saw a man named Matthew sitting at the tax collector's booth. "Follow me," he told him, and Matthew got up and followed him.

While Jesus was having dinner at Matthew's house, many tax collectors and "sinners" came and ate with him and his disciples. When the Pharisees saw this, they asked his disciples, "Why does your teacher eat with tax collectors and 'sinners'?"

On hearing this, Jesus said, "It is not the healthy who need a doctor, but the sick. But go and learn what this means: 'I desire mercy, not sacrifice.' For I have not come to call the righteous, but sinners."

In other words: Jesus associated with "sinners," even though it caused some people to question his reputation, because he wanted them to know the love of God.

2 Peter 2:7–8
Lot, a righteous man, . . . was distressed by the filthy lives of lawless men (for that righteous man, living among them day after day, was tormented in his righteous soul by the lawless deeds he saw and heard).

In other words: Lot associated with "sinners" and it deeply (and adversely) affected his life.

What's the point? We must reach out to unbelievers, but we must be very careful and know our limitations.

Life Changers

- Share the above dilemma with your parents and/or your youth pastor. Ask their advice on how to handle potentially dangerous, potentially compromising situations.
- Ask God for opportunities to talk to your non-Christian friends about Christ.

Cozy Accommodations

Only four more days until Karen and thirty-four other members of the graduating class of Buckner High School leave for their senior trip to South Padre Island. Each participant has been planning and saving and dreaming about this "once-in-a-lifetime" occasion for months now. The thought of being fourteen hours away from home, on their own, on the beach, with a bunch of friends is almost too much to comprehend. A couple of the girls in the group already have their suitcases packed!

But despite all her excitement, Karen is apprehensive. She's heard the stories about what happened on last year's senior trip. She knows many of her classmates, even a few of her church friends, intend to break new ground in the "partying" department. And what has Karen *most* concerned (and what her mom would go nuts over if she only knew!) is the accommodation situation. To cut costs the group has rented three motel rooms right on the beach and a five-bedroom house about 300 yards from the water. Basically, people will be staying wherever they want, which means guys and girls spending the night together.

Karen is bothered by what might happen, by how things will look, and by what she, as a Christian, ought to do.

Thought Joggers

- Is Karen right to be concerned? Why or why not?

- How important is it for Christians to avoid the appearance of evil? What are some practical ways to do this?
- What are some of the potential dangers in a housing arrangement such as the one described above?
- How might Karen extricate herself from the delicate situation she's in?
- How does the reputation of just one Christian affect God's reputation?

Eye-Openers

Consider what wisdom Karen (or someone in a similar situation) might gain from these two passages:

Proverbs 13:20
He who walks with the wise grows wise,
    but a companion of fools suffers harm.

Romans 13:11–14
And do this, understanding the present time. The hour has come for you to wake up from your slumber, because our salvation is nearer now than when we first believed. The night is nearly over; the day is almost here. So let us put aside the deeds of darkness and put on the armor of light. Let us behave decently, as in the daytime, not in orgies and drunkenness, not in sexual immorality and debauchery, not in dissension and jealousy. Rather, clothe yourselves with the Lord Jesus Christ, and do not think about how to gratify the desires of the sinful nature.

Life Changers

- Before you go on a senior trip (or any trip where you might be seriously tempted), sit down with a Christian friend and discuss your values and convictions. Pray together for the strength to do what is right and to avoid what is wrong.
- Talk to your parents about what they did when they were your age and faced similar situations.

Dormitory Pranks

Returning from a late-night date, Dan finds the halls of Neilson Dormitory quiet and empty. Empty, that is, except for one large, plastic container leaning against the door to Room 239. As Dan passes by, he notices that the container is filled with water. Whenever those inside try to leave the room, they're going to be swamped by a small-scale tidal wave!

Entering his own room, Dan finds his roommate Cliff lying on the bed, headphones on, smiling. Cliff sits up, removes the headphones, and says excitedly, "Did you see what I did to Tyler?"

"*You* did that?"

"Yeah. Isn't it great!"

"Well, it couldn't happen to a more deserving guy . . . but Cliff, uh, that's a lot of water. What if Tyler's got electrical stuff on his floor? What if the hall director catches you?"

"Dan, you worry too much. It's just a prank! That's what college dorm life is all about."

Dan drops the subject, but he can't get the situation out of his mind. Cliff doesn't mean to be destructive, but the prank he's pulled could have serious consequences. When Cliff finally drops off to sleep, Dan seriously considers slipping into the hall and disarming the booby trap.

Thought Joggers

- When does a prank cross the line between "harmless/fun" and "harmful/mean"?

- What are Dan's best options?
- What do you think you would do in such a situation?

Eye-Openers

Consider the wisdom in the following passages given to Dan or anyone else who wants to have fun without crossing the line.

The need for wisdom:

Proverbs 10:23
A fool finds pleasure in evil conduct,
    but a man of understanding delights in wisdom.

Proverbs 13:16
Every prudent man acts out of knowledge,
    but a fool exposes his folly.

James 1:5
If any of you lacks wisdom, he should ask God, who gives generously to all without finding fault, and it will be given to him.

James 3:13
Who is wise and understanding among you? Let him show it by his good life, by deeds done in the humility that comes from wisdom.

James 3:17
But the wisdom that comes from heaven is first of all pure; then peace-loving, considerate, submissive, full of mercy and good fruit, impartial and sincere.

The need to consider others:

Philippians 2:4
Each of you should look not only to your own interests, but also to the interests of others.

Life Changers

- Ask your parents to tell you about the funniest, harmless pranks they remember from college.
- Ask God to give you the wisdom to be able to distinguish between good, clean fun and unwise behavior.

Drinking Dilemma

It's Wednesday afternoon and Samantha and her new roommates are moving into their dorm room, unpacking boxes, and making small talk. Between trips to and from the parking lot, the girls are discussing their hometowns, their majors, and the cute guys in the dorm next door, when suddenly Jennifer turns to Samantha and asks point blank, "So, do you drink?"

Samantha is caught completely off guard. She really *doesn't* drink, her one "big" experience with alcohol being the time she had a glass of wine at a cousin's wedding the summer before her senior year. But with both Jennifer and Leigh standing there staring at her (and looking as though they expect a "yes" response), Samantha hears herself reply, "Um, yeah. I mean, I'm not a *heavy* drinker or anything, but sure."

Leigh seems relieved. "Cool. Then, you'd like to come with us to Mother's tonight?"

Samantha is confused. "Mother's?"

Jennifer explains. "Mother's is a bar near campus where a lot of students hang out. They have bands there and people dance. It's pretty fun."

"Um, sure, I'll go with you," Samantha mumbles.

Later Samantha can't believe the situation she's gotten herself into. She's made plans to go out drinking with two girls she barely knows to some bar where God only knows *what* goes on! Suddenly it dawns on her that while she's hanging out in a local bar her family 250 miles back home will be sitting in church!

Samantha feels awful!

Thought Joggers

- Why do you think Samantha lied to her new roommates?
- If a person doesn't get *drunk*, what is wrong with drinking?
- What are your personal convictions when it comes to the issue of alcohol?
- How can individuals avoid getting themselves into the kind of situation in which Samantha finds herself?

Eye-Openers

Consider these biblical principles that relate to the subject above:

Proverbs 23:29–35

Who has woe? Who has sorrow?
  Who has strife? Who has complaints?
  Who has needless bruises? Who has
    bloodshot eyes?
Those who linger over wine,
  who go to sample bowls of mixed wine.
Do not gaze at wine when it is red,
  when it sparkles in the cup,
  when it goes down smoothly!
In the end it bites like a snake
  and poisons like a viper.

Your eyes will see strange sights
and your mind imagine confusing things.
You will be like one sleeping on the high seas,
lying on top of the rigging.
"They hit me," you will say, "but I'm not hurt!
They beat me, but I don't feel it!
When will I wake up
so I can find another drink?"

In other words: Drinking can and does get people into trouble.

1 Corinthians 6:12
"Everything is permissible for me"—but not everything is beneficial. "Everything is permissible for me"—but I will not be mastered by anything.

In other words: Even though Christians have certain freedoms, they must be extremely careful.

Life Changers

- Talk it over with your parents, your youth pastor, your Christian friends, but decide *now* (if you haven't already) what your convictions are in the area of alcohol. The pressures to drink will continue and (likely) increase once you are out of high school. Without firm convictions in this area, you will be swayed as Samantha was.
- Memorize Ephesians 5:18.

Kids Eat Free!

It's early evening on a glorious fall day. Peter, Cary, and four older fraternity brothers are at Sancho Panza's, a Mexican restaurant that's extremely popular with the college crowd. The guys had to wait about forty minutes for a table, but they were rewarded for their patience. The (very attractive) hostess seated them under the sidewalk canopy. From here the guys can view the action in the park across the street. They're rating girls and laughing hard at the expense of one especially clumsy in-line skater.

After putting away several orders of nachos and fajitas (not to mention enough chips to fill a small pickup truck), Ryan, one of the older guys, says to Peter, "Watch this."

He gets up and walks over to a waiter's station, whereupon he casually upsets an entire tray of filled water glasses. Every head in the restaurant whirls around at the sound of the crash. Waiters, busboys, and waitresses rush over to inspect the damage.

Quietly and smoothly, while no one is watching, the three older fraternity guys mumble something about "kids eat free." Then they hop the three-foot railing next to their table, walk hurriedly across the street, and disappear into the park.

All of this happens in the span of about ten seconds. Peter and Cary are stunned. If they run, they're breaking the law. If they sit there, they get stuck with the whole bill. If they turn in their brothers, they'll be black-balled by the rest of the guys in the fraternity.

Peter looks at Cary as though to say, "What are we going to do?"

Cary slides out of his chair and moves nervously toward the railing.

Thought Joggers

- Why would someone who can afford to pay for something try to get it for free?
- Do you know anyone who has ever "skated" (i.e., left a restaurant without paying the bill)? What happened?
- What should Peter and Cary do?
- What do you think you might do in a similar situation?
- If you saw someone stealing something or being dishonest, would you turn him or her in? Why or why not?

Eye-Openers

Consider these biblical principles that relate to the subject above:

Leviticus 19:11
Do not steal. Do not lie. Do not deceive one another.

In other words: Stealing is wrong.

Exodus 23:2
Do not follow the crowd in doing wrong.

1 Corinthians 15:33
Do not be misled: "Bad company corrupts good character."

In other words: The wrong friends can pressure you into doing things that are wrong.

Hebrews 10:24
And let us consider how we may spur one another on toward love and good deeds.

In other words: Christian friends will encourage you to do what is right.

Life Changers

- Before you go out with a group of friends, consider your plans and try to imagine all the things that might happen. Play the "What if?" game. That's where you ask yourself questions like, What will I do if someone tries to ———? or What will I do if someone suggests we ———? A few minutes of thought may spare you a lifetime of grief.
- Get in the habit of speaking the truth in love. Ask God for the courage to look your friends in the eye and tell them what you really think. (If you don't feel the freedom to share your honest thoughts and convictions and feelings with your friends, then they're not very good friends.)

To Pledge or Not?

Brandon is walking through the student union when he spies a bright yellow flyer in the center of a bulletin board. It reads:

FRESHMEN GUYS!
Fraternity Rush Party
Friday, September 6, 7 P.M.
Gamma Omicron Delta Lodge

Brandon stops, scratches his head, and thinks to himself: *Who do I know who's in that fraternity? Oh, yeah, Randy. Maybe I'll give him a call and find out what's up.*

Randy, a junior at State U., is from Brandon's hometown (and church). Since he happens to be the fraternity's rush chairman, he's delighted when Brandon calls for more information.

"Hey, man, I'm so glad you called! Look, I'll give it to you straight. Me and three other guys in the fraternity have been praying all summer about trying to rush some strong Christians. We really want to see God do something in our chapter. We've got a lot of good guys, but only a handful of Christians. So part of our plan is to go out and find some freshmen who love the Lord and want to help us reach out."

Brandon is surprised. "That's kind of weird to hear you talk like that. I mean, it's great and all. I guess I just always kind of thought of fraternities as being these wild groups of guys who just drink and party all the time."

Randy laughs. "Well, we certainly have our share of those kinds of folks. But think about it this way—they need Christ as much as anybody. Who's gonna reach 'em if we don't?"

"Well, yeah, I guess I see your point, but isn't it hard to live for Christ in that environment? I mean, you must have a million temptations all around you!"

"Absolutely. It is tough. And that's all the more reason why we need to get a good core group of believers, so that we can be strong and hold each other accountable."

Brandon is confused. He's always assumed that fraternities are evil and that Christians should stay completely away. Now he's not so sure.

Thought Joggers

- What do *you* think about fraternities and sororities? Why?
- What would be good reasons or motives to join a social fraternity? What would you consider lame reasons?
- Do you think Randy is sincere about his desire to reach his fraternity brothers, or are his words just a form of rationalization?
- What would be the potential dangers of getting involved with a group of nonbelievers?
- What should Brandon do?

Eye-Openers

Consider the following Bible passage from 2 Corinthians 5 and how it might relate to Brandon's decision:

For we must all appear before the judgment seat of Christ, that each one may receive what is due him for the things done while in the body, whether good or bad.

Since, then, we know what it is to fear the Lord, we try to persuade men. What we are is plain to God, and I hope it is also plain to your conscience. We are not trying to commend ourselves to you again, but are giving you an opportunity to take pride in us, so that you can answer those who take pride in what is seen rather than in what is in the heart. If we are out of our mind, it is for the sake of God; if we are in our right mind, it is for you. For Christ's love compels us, because we are convinced that one died for all, and therefore all died. And he died for all, that those who live should no longer live for themselves but for him who died for them and was raised again.

So from now on we regard no one from a worldly point of view. Though we once regarded Christ in this way, we do so no longer. Therefore, if anyone is in Christ, he is a new creation; the old has gone, the new has come! All this is from God, who reconciled us to himself through Christ and gave us the ministry of reconciliation: that God was reconciling the world to himself in Christ, not counting men's sins against them. And he has committed to us the message of reconciliation. We are therefore Christ's ambassadors, as though God were making his appeal through us. We implore you on Christ's behalf: Be reconciled to God. God made him who had no sin to be sin for us, so that in him we might become the righteousness of God.

Life Changers

- Make your own "Ten Most Wanted" list. That's a list of ten friends, neighbors, or family members who do not know Christ. Keep the list in your wallet and pray for their salvation daily.
- Before you join *any* group or organization, talk it over with Christian friends who know your strengths and vulnerabilities. Ask them for some honest feedback.

Basic Training Blues

With average grades and very little money in savings, Ray figured a two-year hitch in the army might be his best move after high school. So now he finds himself in the blazing summer heat at Ft. LeMat, counting the days remaining in basic training.

Apart from the early wake-up calls, Ray hasn't found military life too terrible. High school football workouts were a lot more taxing than the physical training required by the army. The food is better than he expected. Add to that the fact that most of the guys in his platoon are cool. All in all, it's been a pretty good experience.

There is one recruit, however, who's having an especially rough time. His name is Cliff. He's overweight and he has one of those personalities where people just naturally like to pick on him.

Tonight in the showers, a bunch of the guys grabbed Cliff with the intent of humiliating him. (Good taste forbids a description of their plan—use your imagination.) Ray watched from across the way and felt torn inside. Part of him wanted to laugh; something else within him wanted to tell the guys to knock it off.

Ray hesitated for a few moments and then walked away. He reasoned that if he tried to intervene, he'd just end up ticking everybody off.

Later that evening after everyone was asleep, Ray got out of bed to go to the rest room. When he passed Cliff's bunk, he heard a muffled sob.

Thought Joggers

- Why do some people seem to be a constant target or "magnet" for verbal and emotional abuse?
- Why is it that basically "nice" individuals will sometimes do things in a group that are definitely "not nice"?
- Have you ever tried to stand up for someone who was being persecuted or ridiculed? What happened?
- What, if anything, can Ray do to change the situation he finds himself in?
- How do you typically respond when the crowd is urging you to join in their action?

Eye-Openers

Consider the way Christians are to live—especially in relationship to other people:

Colossians 3:12
Therefore, as God's chosen people, holy and dearly loved, clothe yourselves with compassion, kindness, humility, gentleness and patience.

In other words: We are to be Christlike.

1 Thessalonians 5:14–15
And we urge you, brothers, warn those who are idle, encourage the timid, help the weak, be patient with everyone. Make sure that nobody pays back wrong for wrong, but always try to be kind to each other and to everyone else.

In other words: We are to look out for the less fortunate.

Galatians 5:22–23
But the fruit of the Spirit is love, joy, peace, patience, kindness, goodness, faithfulness, gentleness and self-control. Against such things there is no law.

In other words: We can live as we should through the power of the Holy Spirit.

Life Changers

- Ask God to give you a heart that feels empathy and compassion for those who are hurting.
- Ask a close friend to evaluate or grade you in the areas of gentleness, kindness, compassion, and courage in standing up for the truth.
- Read the Gospel of Mark and notice how Jesus dealt with the people he encountered.

Breaking Up

It's early June and Kevin is lying by the pool, soaking up the sun. His thoughts alternate between the happy memory of graduation night just a few weeks before and the eager expectation of going off to college in a couple of months.

He's heard stories about university life, and he's seen a few movies that feature the wild antics of college students. If he could, he'd pack up and leave today—that's how ready he is to get out of Simmsport.

As he rolls over to catch some rays on his back, he spies Mandi on the other side of the pool. Seeing her makes him think of Kacey, which reminds him of Shonda, which ultimately leads him to think of Ellen, his girlfriend.

He and Ellen have been dating for a year. She's a great girl, and he likes her a lot. Problem is, she's only a sophomore. So Kevin has a big decision to make: Is he going to stay together with Ellen—trying to date her long-distance—and come home every other weekend? Or is he going to break up with her so that they can each get on with life?

Though he isn't totally sure what the state university will be like, the idea of leaving the grown-up, exciting world of college to come back to "juvenile, small-town" events like proms and high school football games doesn't exactly thrill him.

At the same time, he wonders if breaking up is wise. Ellen is a sweet Christian girl and she likes him a lot. It's kind of nice to always have someone to do things with. His friends would think he was crazy if he dumped her.

Kevin shrugs to himself, picks up the copy of *Sports Illustrated* beneath his chair, and starts reading about the NBA finals.

Thought Joggers

- What are the positives and negatives of a high school graduate dating someone who is still in high school?
- What advice would you give Kevin if he asked for your opinion?
- What are some legitimate and illegitimate reasons for ending a dating relationship?
- Would it be possible for Kevin and Ellen to go out when he is home, and yet date other people when they are separated? Why or why not?
- What would you do in a situation like this?

Eye-Openers

The following Scriptures offer practical principles for those who find themselves in a situation similar to Kevin and Ellen's:

James 1:5
If any of you lacks wisdom, he should ask God, who gives generously to all without finding fault, and it will be given to him.

In other words: God promises to guide us.

1 Corinthians 13:4–8
Love is patient, love is kind. It does not envy, it does not boast, it is not proud. It is not rude, it is not self-seeking, it is not easily angered, it keeps no record of wrongs. Love does not delight in evil but rejoices with the truth. It always protects, always trusts, always hopes, always perseveres.
    Love never fails. But where there are prophecies, they will cease; where there are tongues, they will be stilled; where there is knowledge, it will pass away.

In other words: True love seeks what is best for the other person.

Proverbs 15:22
Plans fail for lack of counsel,
    but with many advisers they succeed.

In other words: Before making big decisions, seek the advice of wise counselors.

Life Changers

- To get a realistic picture of what it is like to continue dating someone in high school after you have graduated, talk to several couples in this situation.
- Read the story of Abram in Genesis 12. As you do, recognize that God asked him to do something that his friends and neighbors must have thought was crazy—let go of a sure thing (living in Ur) for something unknown (traveling to a mysterious, distant land). After you have read this story, ask God to give you the faith to live like Abram.

Dating and Relating

Dana's parents first allowed her to date at age sixteen. Their big rules? One, *no* dating non-Christians. Two, no *dating* non-Christians. And three, no dating *non-Christians*. In case you haven't guessed, the Madlocks would prefer that their daughter date young men who share their daughter's spiritual beliefs.

Now that Dana has moved away from home, she has a lot more freedom and independence. She is reexamining her convictions and making her own decisions.

Here's the dilemma Dana's facing this weekend: She met a guy named Wayne at a party last Saturday night. He's a little bit older. He's apparently got a good job. He seems really nice. And he is *very* nice looking.

Wayne called Dana Sunday, Monday, and Tuesday nights. They talked and laughed together for hours on the phone each night. On Monday they briefly talked about the subject of church and religious beliefs. Wayne basically said, "I *do* believe in God, but I *don't* know if I think the Bible is 100 percent accurate, and I definitely feel *very* uncomfortable in church." That comment disappointed Dana, but everything else about their conversations has been wonderful. There seems to be a "spark" or "connection" developing between the two.

Now it's Wednesday night and Wayne has just asked Dana to go out to dinner on Saturday night. In the back of her mind she thinks momentarily about her parents and about Wayne's disinterest in spiritual things; in the next second she thinks about how much fun he is to talk to.

"I'd love to go out with you, Wayne," she responds.

Thought Joggers

- If you're not talking "marriage," what's the big deal about going out once or twice with a nice non-Christian?
- What are the potential problems for Christians and non-Christians when they date?
- Second Corinthians 5 *encourages* us to build relationships with unbelievers; the next chapter *discourages* us from intimate relationships with unbelievers. Why isn't this a contradiction?
- What if a Christian girl never gets asked out by a Christian guy, but only by non-Christians? What is she supposed to do?
- What do you think about Dana's decision? What would you likely do in a similar situation?

Eye-Openers

The Bible offers us valuable insights about dating and relating:

2 Corinthians 6:14–16
Do not be yoked together with unbelievers. For what do righteousness and wickedness have in common? Or what fellowship can light have with darkness? What harmony is there between Christ and Belial? What does a believer have in common with an unbeliever? What agreement is there between the temple of God and idols?

For we are the temple of the living God. As God has said:
"I will live with them and walk among them, and I will
be their God, and they will be my people."

In other words: Intimate relationships with unbelievers bring trouble and heartache.

Proverbs 7:6–23

At the window of my house
    I looked out through the lattice.
I saw among the simple,
    I noticed among the young men,
    a youth who lacked judgment.
He was going down the street near her corner,
    walking along in the direction of her house
at twilight, as the day was fading,
    as the dark of night set in.
Then out came a woman to meet him,
    dressed like a prostitute and with crafty intent.
(She is loud and defiant,
    her feet never stay at home;
now in the street, now in the squares,
    at every corner she lurks.)
She took hold of him and kissed him
    and with a brazen face she said:
"I have fellowship offerings at home;
    today I fulfilled my vows.
So I came out to meet you;
    I looked for you and have found you!
I have covered my bed
    with colored linens from Egypt.
I have perfumed my bed
    with myrrh, aloes and cinnamon.
Come, let's drink deep of love till morning;
    let's enjoy ourselves with love!

My husband is not at home;
>he has gone on a long journey.
He took his purse filled with money
>and will not be home till full moon."
With persuasive words she led him astray;
>she seduced him with her smooth talk.
All at once he followed her
>like an ox going to the slaughter,
like a deer stepping into a noose
>till an arrow pierces his liver,
like a bird darting into a snare,
>little knowing it will cost him his life.

In other words: God's wisdom is necessary if we are to avoid getting into bad relationships with the wrong people.

Life Changers

- Talk to some of the women in your church whom you respect. Ask them to relate their experiences to you about dating and relating to guys who don't seem to be interested in Christ.
- Read 1 Kings 11 and note what happened to King Solomon when he became intimate with women who did not share his spiritual beliefs.
- Begin praying daily for God to lead you in his time and according to his will in your dating life.

My Stuff, Your Stuff

Melinda and Carrie have a pretty good roommate relationship except for one thing: Melinda goes overboard with borrowing Carrie's things. Clothes, food, CDs—you name it, and if Carrie isn't wearing it, chewing it, or listening to it *at that very moment*, Melinda feels the freedom to borrow it—usually without asking.

Today Carrie invited Pam to come over after work and eat some leftover egg rolls, fried rice, and sweet and sour chicken (from dinner the night before). When Carrie opened the refrigerator, the Chinese food was nowhere to be seen. In the garbage can were two big styrofoam take-out boxes dripping with soy sauce.

"She did it again!" Carrie hissed under her breath.

"What?" Pam was clueless.

"It's Melinda! She does this to me at least once a week. I get my mouth set for something, and I come home all ready to eat it, and it's gone! She eats all my food! She not only ate this without asking, but she ate all of it!"

"Why don't you eat *her* food?"

"What food? She doesn't *buy* food, because she doesn't have to. Why should she? She can just eat *my* stuff!"

"Why don't you say something to her?"

Carrie's mood softens. "I guess I probably should, but I just feel sorry for her. She's struggling to get by. My job pays more, plus I get some help from my parents. But Melinda—she's all on her own. She barely makes enough to pay the rent. I'd feel like a dog telling her to leave my stuff alone."

"Gosh, Carrie, you're a lot nicer than I would be."

"If you knew how mad I sometimes get on the inside, you wouldn't say that. I guess the truth is I'm pretty selfish."

Thought Joggers

- What do you think about the Carrie-Melinda living situation? Does it seem fair to you? Do you think Carrie is selfish?
- Should Carrie keep her mouth shut? Should she confront Melinda? If she decided to speak up, how could she do so in a loving fashion?
- Do you tend to borrow from others more often, or do others generally borrow from you? Why do you think this is so?
- In a perfect world, how would roommates resolve the borrowing problem?
- The Bible encourages generosity, but it also stresses honesty. How do we comply with both of those commands in a situation like the one above?
- What possessions would you not want to loan out? Why?

Eye-Openers

Consider a few biblical examples that speak to Melinda and Carrie's situation:

Psalm 24:1
The earth is the LORD's, and everything in it,
the world, and all who live in it.

In other words: God is the actual owner of everything we have.

1 Timothy 6:18
Command them [those who can afford to share] to do good, to be rich in good deeds, and to be generous and willing to share.

In other words: We are to be generous with our possessions.

Psalm 112:5
Good will come to him who is generous and lends freely,
    who conducts his affairs with justice.

Proverbs 11:25
A generous man will prosper;
    he who refreshes others will himself be refreshed.

In other words: We are blessed when we share with others.

Life Changers

- It's not so much what we give, but how we give that counts. Second Corinthians emphasizes cheerfulness in sharing with others. Ask God to make you more willing to share, and more cheerful when you do.
- Make sure you possess your *things,* and they don't possess *you.* A good warning sign of greed or materialism is when you become more concerned about your possessions than you are about the people in your life.

Dating Heaven

Heather had her share of dates in high school, but *nothing* like she's experienced so far in college. Her phone has been ringing nonstop!

Today she has set a new personal record (and for all we know a school record too)—three separate dates with three different guys! At noon she's got a lunch date with Ryan. At three she's supposed to play racquetball with Walter. At seven Jack's picking her up to go to a fraternity function.

Mid-afternoon, after Heather rushes out in her sweats to meet Walter, her suitemates have the following discussion:

Amanda: I can't believe how lucky she is. I get maybe one date a month. She's got three in one day!

Stephanie: Well, I think she's messing up!

Amanda: Do I detect a little jealousy?

Stephanie: No! I just think she's wrong to play with those guys' emotions.

Amanda: How?

Stephanie: Well, I don't know about Ryan, but I know for a fact that Walter and Jack both really like her. And I'm pretty sure they don't know she's seeing them both. How do you think Jack would feel if, when he picked her up tonight, he found out she'd already been out with two other guys—just today?!

Amanda: Serves him right! He's too full of himself anyway! Besides, I've known plenty of guys who want to "play the field." Why is it so wrong when a girl wants to do it?

Thought Joggers

- (Girls) What do you think about Heather's behavior?
- (Guys) What do you think about Heather's behavior?
- Comment on the argument that Heather should only go out with one guy at a time because she might hurt someone's feelings.
- Comment on the argument that Heather is free to do whatever she wants as long as she doesn't lie or mislead any of the guys who are interested in her.
- If you were Heather's friend, what, if anything, would you say to her?

Eye-Openers

There are no Scriptures that give explicit "rules for *dating,*" but there are Scriptures that give explicit "rules for *relating.*" Take Romans 12 for example:

Therefore, I urge you, brothers, in view of God's mercy, to offer your bodies as living sacrifices, holy and pleasing to God—this is your spiritual act of worship. Do not conform any longer to the pattern of this world, but be transformed by the renewing of your mind. Then you will be able to test and approve what God's will is—his good, pleasing and perfect will.

For by the grace given me I say to every one of you: Do not think of yourself more highly than you ought, but rather think of yourself with sober judgment, in accordance with the measure of faith God has given you. Just as each of us has one body with many members, and these members do not all have the same function, so in Christ we who are many form one body, and each member belongs to all the others. We have different gifts, according to the grace given us. If a man's gift is prophesying, let him use it in proportion to his faith. If it is serving, let him serve; if it is teaching, let him teach; if it is encouraging, let him encourage; if it is contributing to the needs of others, let him give generously; if it is leadership, let him govern diligently; if it is showing mercy, let him do it cheerfully.

Love must be sincere. Hate what is evil; cling to what is good. Be devoted to one another in brotherly love. Honor one another above yourselves. Never be lacking in zeal, but keep your spiritual fervor, serving the Lord. Be joyful in hope, patient in affliction, faithful in prayer. Share with God's people who are in need. Practice hospitality.

Bless those who persecute you; bless and do not curse. Rejoice with those who rejoice; mourn with those who mourn. Live in harmony with one another. Do not be proud, but be willing to associate with people of low position. Do not be conceited. Do not repay anyone evil for evil. Be careful to do what is right in the eyes of everybody. If it is possible, as far as it depends on you, live at peace with everyone. Do not take revenge, my friends, but leave room for God's wrath, for it is written: "It is mine to avenge; I will repay," says the Lord. On the contrary: "If your enemy is hungry, feed him; if he is thirsty, give him something to drink. In doing this, you will heap burning coals on his head."

Do not be overcome by evil, but overcome evil with good.

Life Changers

- A lot of people these days are writing their own life purpose statements (a document that summa rizes one's goals and purpose in life). Why not write your own *dating* purpose statement? Put on paper your standards for why, when, where, how, and whom you will date.
- Focus less on dating and more on friendship, and you'll experience a lot less stress and anxiety. (Note: It is much easier to transition from a friend relationship into a dating relationship than to transform a romance into a mere friendship.)
- Share the story above with two male friends and two female friends and evaluate their responses.

Dumping a Date

All through high school, even when everyone else was being mean to Tayler, Meredith treated him with gentleness and kindness.

"Why do you pick on him?" she would chide her friends. "I mean, I know he's kind of goofy, but he's not bothering *you*. Just leave him alone."

Even though they're now college freshmen, Meredith still feels protective of her awkward friend. Something about him, she doesn't know what, brings out in her a never-before-seen "maternal instinct."

Last weekend, Meredith's kindness came back to haunt her. The phone rang, and it was Tayler. Before Meredith even realized what was happening or what she was saying, she heard herself agreeing to go with him to Homecoming.

All week she has been kicking herself. To make matters worse, when she got back from the library tonight, there was a message from Patrick on her answering machine. Meredith feels confident (based on a conversation she had with one of Patrick's friends) that he was calling to ask her to Homecoming.

So there's her dilemma: She can go on a "mercy date" with Tayler or she can break the date with him and go with Patrick, the guy she's really interested in getting to know.

Thought Joggers

- Evaluate Meredith's attitudes and actions toward Tayler (including her desire to break the date with him). How would you grade her behavior?

- Estimate the impact on Tayler if Meredith breaks their date in order to go out with Patrick.
- Which is worse: the breaking of a commitment (Meredith's calling off the date with Tayler) or hypocrisy (Meredith's going out with a guy she doesn't want to be with)? What other options does Meredith have?
- How should Christians handle invitations they do not wish to accept?
- What would you counsel Meredith to do?

Eye-Openers

Psalm 15 has a lot to say about Meredith's situation. Read this psalm of David carefully, noting its promises to those who obey its commands:

LORD, who may dwell in your sanctuary?
    Who may live on your holy hill?
He whose walk is blameless
    and who does what is righteous,
who speaks the truth from his heart
    and has no slander on his tongue,
who does his neighbor no wrong
    and casts no slur on his fellow man,
who despises a vile man
    but honors those who fear the LORD,
who keeps his oath
    even when it hurts,
who lends his money without usury
    and does not accept a bribe against the innocent.

He who does these things
will never be shaken.

Life Changers

- Sit down with a Christian friend and role-play
  what you would say in a situation similar to the
  one above. Make sure that your words are truthful and tender.
- Take a page from Meredith's book—befriend
  someone whom everyone else tends to pick on or
  ignore. We are most like Jesus when we reach out
  in love and compassion to those who are ignored
  or rejected.

Noisy Neighbors

Just as Lynn and Patti are drifting off to sleep, they are jarred (once again) by the sounds of loud music coming through the walls from next door. Lynn bolts upright in bed, clicks on the light, and stares angrily at Patti. Patti returns a glare that could melt the polar ice caps.

"This is ridiculous!" Lynn hisses.

"That's it! I'm gonna beat on the wall and tell them to turn it down!"

Lynn softens, "No, don't. If we get mad and yell and make a big fuss, then we'll blow our Christian witness. It's been hard enough just trying to become friends with those girls. Let's don't blow it."

"Well, we've got to think of something!" Patti declares. "I can't live like this. I've got an eight o'clock class. Call the apartment manager."

"She's not going to do anything. People call and complain to her all the time. She'd go knock on their door and say, 'Turn down your music,' and they would . . . until she got back in her apartment. Then they'd crank it right back up."

"So what are we going to do?"

Lynn tries to lighten the mood. "We could buy earplugs?"

"Very funny!" Patti fumes.

"All right, look . . . what if we just go over there and talk to them?"

"Talk to them?! Are you serious?!"

"You got any better ideas?"
"What would we *say*?"
"Good question."

Thought Joggers

- What disputes with neighbors have you had (or observed) in your life? What happened?
- What are Lynn and Patti's best options?
- If Lynn and Patti do in fact go next door and talk to their neighbors, what would you advise them to say and why?
- Does being a Christian mean that you have to let others take advantage of you and trample on your rights?
- What would you do in a situation like the one described above?

Eye-Openers

Consider these Bible passages and principles:

Philippians 2:3

Do nothing out of selfish ambition or vain conceit, but in humility consider others better than yourselves.

In other words: We are to think of others first.

Acts 25:10–11

Paul answered: "I am now standing before Caesar's court, where I ought to be tried. I have not done any wrong to the Jews, as you yourself know very well. If, however, I am guilty of doing anything deserving death,

I do not refuse to die. But if the charges brought against me by these Jews are not true, no one has the right to hand me over to them. I appeal to Caesar!"

In other words: There are times when it is legitimate to stand up for our rights.

Matthew 5:14–16
You are the light of the world. A city on a hill cannot be hidden. Neither do people light a lamp and put it under a bowl. Instead they put it on its stand, and it gives light to everyone in the house. In the same way, let your light shine before men, that they may see your good deeds and praise your Father in heaven.

In other words: As long as our responses and actions are godly, we will be good witnesses.

Life Changers

- Make the effort when you first move into a new place to get to know your neighbors. It is a whole lot easier to discuss problems with a friend than with a stranger!
- Moses was known as the most humble man on earth. And yet read how firmly and truthfully he dealt with Pharaoh in Exodus 5–10.
- Compare Jesus' reaction upon being struck (John 18:19–24) with the apostle Paul's reaction (Acts 23:1–3).

The Marriage Muddle

Recent high school graduates Doug and Julie are talking seriously about the *M* word—*M* as in marriage, matrimony, and marital bliss. Such discussion shouldn't surprise anyone. The two have been sweethearts since ninth grade. Both are Christians and members of a good church. As far as dating relationships go, theirs is one of the more solid ones. But when Julie's mom found a copy of *Beautiful Bride* magazine in her bedroom a few minutes ago, she hit the roof.

"Julie, you are way too young to be thinking about this!"

"Mom, you were only nineteen when you and Dad got married!"

"That's different!"

"How?"

"Well, for starters, your father was twenty-two."

"But, Mom, you've said yourself that you and Dad love Doug. That you think he's great."

"We do. We do. But we also don't want to see you two jump into this thing without thinking. Marriage is tough, even when two people are crazy about each other—even when they're a lot older and wiser."

"Mom, there are a lot of things I don't know about marriage. But I do know what the word *commitment* means. And I also know that I love Doug, and I want to spend my life with him. We want to be together . . . Mom, don't you remember what that's like? Mom, I know this will probably freak you out, but we want to sleep together! We haven't done that, but sometimes we want to so much it almost aches."

Mrs. Naylor is silent.

Julie continues, "The Bible says wait. Well, Mom, we've been waiting for more than three years, and it just keeps getting harder and harder. Doesn't the Bible say it's better to marry than to burn with passion?"

"Well, uh, yes it does say that. But that by itself is not a good enough reason to start planning a wedding."

"Oh, Mom, it's more than that."

"Honey, look . . . I'm just so surprised and shocked by all this, I can't even think straight. You're my baby! Can we wait and talk to your dad when he gets home?"

"I guess so."

Thought Joggers

- What are the pros and cons of marrying at an early age?
- Why are so many people (even people from terrible family situations) so eager to get married so soon?
- What are good reasons and not-so-good reasons for getting married?
- What advice would you give to Doug and Julie if they came to you for counseling?

Eye-Openers

Consider the description of the kind of marital love that pleases God in this passage from Ephesians 5:22–23:

Wives, submit to your husbands as to the Lord. For the husband is the head of the wife as Christ is the head of the church, his body, of which he is the Savior. Now as the church submits to Christ, so also wives should submit to their husbands in everything.

Husbands, love your wives, just as Christ loved the church and gave himself up for her to make her holy, cleansing her by the washing with water through the word, and to present her to himself as a radiant church, without stain or wrinkle or any other blemish, but holy and blameless. In this same way, husbands ought to love their wives as their own bodies. He who loves his wife loves himself. After all, no one ever hated his own body, but he feeds and cares for it, just as Christ does the church—for we are members of his body. "For this reason a man will leave his father and mother and be united to his wife, and the two will become one flesh." This is a profound mystery—but I am talking about Christ and the church. However, each one of you also must love his wife as he loves himself, and the wife must respect her husband.

Life Changers

- Visit your local Christian bookstore or church library and get a book on dating, sex, and marriage (ask your pastor or youth leader to recommend a good title).
- Find a couple in your church that married at a young age. Ask them to tell you about the ups and downs of marrying early.

Roommate Roulette

On his housing form under the section "roommate preference" Daryl checked the box labeled "none." He reasoned, *Hey, it's a Christian college, and I'm a pretty laid-back guy. I can get along with anybody. It won't really matter who I get.*

Wrong.

Daryl was assigned to live with Drew P., a transfer student from the Midwest. Less than seventy-two hours into his new living situation, Daryl realized he had made a huge mistake. Here's a partial list of the problems that have surfaced so far:

- Daryl is a studious guy who likes to hit the sack about 11:00 P.M. and get up no later than 6:00. He's a certified morning person. Drew, on the other hand, likes to watch TV until 1:30 or 2:00 A.M. and sleep in. The first morning Daryl turned his closet light on so that he could pick out some clothes. Drew pulled his blanket over his head and angrily mumbled something like, "Can't you see I'm trying to sleep over here?"
- Two of Daryl's friends mentioned leaving messages with Drew his second night in the dorm. But Daryl never got any messages.
- Drew says he can't sleep unless the window is open. That includes cold evenings like last night when the temperature outside dropped to thirty-

eight! And when Drew does drift off to sleep, he snores like a freight train!

• Finally, according to Daryl, Drew's shoes smell like something crawled up inside them and died!

As you might have guessed, Daryl has an extremely bad attitude toward Drew. He even hates going to his dorm room. "Either *I've* got to move out, or *he* does. But I can't live with this guy for a whole semester. He drives me nuts!"

Thought Joggers

• Evaluate Daryl's living situation. Which circumstance(s) would cause you the most anger and/or frustration?
• Do two people have to be alike (or mostly alike) to get along? Why or why not?
• How come people who are best friends often see their relationship deteriorate when they live together?
• What, in your opinion, are the hardest aspects of rooming with someone?
• Imagine that Daryl comes to you and says, "Help me figure out what to say to this guy." What would you advise him to say to Drew, and how could he say it in a non-offensive way?
• Assume you are a resident advisor and you are trying to help Daryl and Drew talk and work through their differences. Which course of action would you recommend: (1) one or both move out, or (2) they both stay and try to work it out?

Eye-Openers

Consider what principles Colossians 3 mentions that would help Christians in relating to each other:

Since, then, you have been raised with Christ, set your hearts on things above, where Christ is seated at the right hand of God. Set your minds on things above, not on earthly things. For you died, and your life is now hidden with Christ in God. When Christ, who is your life, appears, then you also will appear with him in glory.

Put to death, therefore, whatever belongs to your earthly nature: sexual immorality, impurity, lust, evil desires and greed, which is idolatry. Because of these, the wrath of God is coming. You used to walk in these ways, in the life you once lived. But now you must rid yourselves of all such things as these: anger, rage, malice, slander, and filthy language from your lips. Do not lie to each other, since you have taken off your old self with its practices and have put on the new self, which is being renewed in knowledge in the image of its Creator. Here there is no Greek or Jew, circumcised or uncircumcised, barbarian, Scythian, slave or free, but Christ is all, and is in all.

Therefore, as God's chosen people, holy and dearly loved, clothe yourselves with compassion, kindness, humility, gentleness and patience. Bear with each other and forgive whatever grievances you may have against one another. Forgive as the Lord forgave you. And over all these virtues put on love, which binds them all together in perfect unity.

Let the peace of Christ rule in your hearts, since as members of one body you were called to peace. And be thankful. Let the word of Christ dwell in you richly as you teach and admonish one another with all wisdom, and as you sing psalms, hymns and spiritual songs with gratitude in your hearts to God. And whatever you do, whether in word or deed, do it all in the name of the Lord Jesus, giving thanks to God the Father through him.

Life Changers

- Recognize a couple of important facts. First, conflict is inevitable. Even best friends and roommates have disagreements. Second, conflict is bad only if it is handled badly. The issue isn't *conflict* (you'll always have it), but *the way you resolve your conflicts* (do you follow the guidelines of Scripture in working through them?).
- Ask your parents for their best advice on handling roommate squabbles and disagreements.

The Unsteady Steady

Travis and Tammy have been going out for about a year. Since Tammy is now a college freshman and Travis is a high school senior, there were a few discussions back in the summer about breaking up. But after thinking it over and talking with friends the couple decided to continue their exclusive, steady relationship. It's been inconvenient to date long distance, and the phone bills have been astronomical. Nevertheless, the "Travis and Tammy tandem" has continued on an even keel.

Until about a week ago. That's when Grant entered the picture. Who is Grant? He's a junior pre-law student Tammy met at the church potluck luncheon last weekend when she didn't go home. As Tammy and Grant talked, they realized they have a class together. All this week the two have been *sitting* together. Last night they even *studied* together. Then, when they got through at the library, they went out for coffee at an all-night diner.

Tammy thoroughly enjoyed Grant's mature, sophisticated sense of humor. In fact, the two were having so much fun talking, Tammy completely lost track of time. It wasn't until she got home at 1:15 that she realized she had forgotten she was supposed to be home at 11:00 for Travis's call. (He ended up calling four times.)

Tonight when Tammy called back, Travis was upset. When Tammy casually mentioned that she had been studying with Grant, Travis's hurt turned into hostile anger. He accused her of being unfaithful, of going out with other guys. Then he hung up on her. Sitting there listening to the dial tone, Tammy is miffed at Travis's immature reaction. *I haven't been unfaithful to you,* she thinks. *But when you act like that, you make me want to be!*

Thought Joggers

- Do you think it was wise for Tammy and Travis, in light of their circumstances, to continue an "exclusive dating relationship"?
- Who do you feel more sympathetic for in this story—Tammy or Travis? Why?
- What do you think about Travis's reaction? How might he have better handled the situation?
- Would it be wrong for Tammy to break up with Travis to go out with Grant? Why or why not?
- What would you counsel Tammy to do?
- What would you do if you were Travis? If you were Tammy?

Eye-Openers

First Corinthians 13 is a great reminder of what mature love looks like. If you're going out with someone right now, evaluate your relationship in light of these qualities:

> Love is patient, love is kind. It does not envy, it does not boast, it is not proud. It is not rude, it is not self-seeking, it is not easily angered, it keeps no record of wrongs. Love does not delight in evil but rejoices with the truth. It always protects, always trusts, always hopes, always perseveres.
>
> Love never fails. . . .

Life Changers

- The thought of a steady boyfriend or girlfriend often seems too wonderful to imagine. But balance those romantic (and somewhat unrealistic) images with these facts: Exclusive dating relationships also include the dangerous temptations to forget your friends, become possessive, become overly dependent on another, become jealous, become physically involved, become unhealthily obsessed with marriage, etc.
- Before you commit to any kind of exclusive dating arrangement, you would be extremely wise to consult your best Christian friends and your wisest Christian counselors or advisors. If, after explaining the situation, they think it's a good idea, then you'll have a better chance for success.

"Chucking" Church

For as long as he can remember Greg has been going to church. And not just any church, but a very strict church with numerous rules—and almost as many meetings and services.

Greg is turned off by long, stern sermons on "worldliness." He's tired of feeling guilty all the time. He's had it with feeling like he can never measure up to what God wants. So here's what Greg is thinking: When he graduates in a few months, instead of going to the strict Bible college where his parents went (and where they want him to go), he just may pay a visit to the local Air Force recruiting office.

He reasons this way: "If I join the Air Force, I can get some good training, and then, if I want to go to school later—a college *I* choose—the government will help pay for my education. Plus, who knows! I might even get stationed in some cool place overseas. But the best thing about getting in the military is that I'll be able to make my own decisions—especially about church. If I wake up on Sunday morning and don't want to go, I won't go. No more nagging from my parents, and no more guilt. Man, I gotta do something to get away from all this—I feel like I'm suffocating!"

Thought Joggers

- How many of your friends do you expect will stop going to church once they graduate and go off to college or start living on their own? Why?

- What do you think about Greg's reasoning? Do his plans seem wise, or does it sound to you like he is just trying to escape a bad situation?
- How can parents encourage their kids to grow spiritually without being "preachy" or "pushy"?
- Can you think of other options for Greg? What?
- Is your faith really your own or are you living by a faith that you have merely "borrowed" from your parents?
- What is involved in "owning" your own faith?

Eye-Openers

If, like Greg, you are thinking about "chucking" church, consider this passage from Hebrews 10:23–25:

Let us hold unswervingly to the hope we profess, for he who promised is faithful. And let us consider how we may spur one another on toward love and good deeds. Let us not give up meeting together, as some are in the habit of doing, but let us encourage one another—and all the more as you see the Day approaching.

Life Changers

- It's common for high school graduates and college freshmen (especially those who have grown up in religious homes) to have questions about their faith and about what kind of role church will have in their future. Before you make the radical decision to "chuck" organized religion altogether, at least check out some other Bible-believing churches and evangelical parachurch groups (Campus Crusade for Christ, Fellowship of Christian Athletes, Inter-Varsity, etc.). You just may find a group of Christians who will strengthen your faith and help you see God in a new light.

- Conduct an informal survey, asking your friends what they like and don't like about their churches.
- Read the book of Acts to see what a church can be like when Christians let God work in and through them.

Cult Watch

Shannon figured she might get homesick going off to a school more than 800 miles away. What she didn't count on was the depth of her loneliness. Here's a quick summary of the first week's highlights (or perhaps lowlights is a better word):

- Shannon's roommate is a student from the Middle East who speaks very little English.
- Most of the girls on her dorm floor already seem to know each other. In fact, a big group of them went to high school together, and so they hang out together all the time.
- Four of Shannon's five classes meet in giant auditoriums and have at least 200 students in each one.
- Shannon's bicycle was stolen the second day of classes.
- Shannon's mailbox has been empty six out of seven days.
- She has eaten nineteen of twenty-one meals by herself.

However, last night in the cafeteria, an attractive girl came over, introduced herself as Kim, and asked if she could sit and eat supper with Shannon. Shannon was delighted to have another human being to talk to. "I never knew I would be so lonely in the middle of a campus of 20,000 students!"

Kim smiled and replied, "I know just what you mean."

The two talked for a couple of hours. Then Kim said, "Hey, Shannon, you know what? I'm part of a Christian group on campus called God's Forever Family. You've probably never heard of us, but we have a house right off campus. There are probably fifty or so students involved, and we do a lot of fun stuff. We have retreats and study groups and parties. If you want, I could take you over there and we could play Ping-Pong or something. And I could introduce you around. If nothing else, it would give you a chance to meet some other Christians and let you get out of your room for a while."

There's something really different about her, Shannon thinks to herself. *She's the first sweet person I've met.*

"Sure!" Shannon replies. "I'd love to meet your friends."

Thought Joggers

- Why do you think so many people (even people from Christian backgrounds) get involved with cults?
- How can Christians guard against being deceived?
- Kim comes across as really sweet and caring. How can Shannon know if Kim's group, God's Forever Family, is an orthodox Christian group?
- What should Christians do before they get too involved in any group?

Eye-Openers

Consider the following Bible passages that warn against false teachers:

2 Peter 2:1–3

But there were also false prophets among the people, just as there will be false teachers among you. They will secretly introduce destructive heresies, even denying the sovereign Lord who bought them—bringing swift destruction on themselves. Many will follow their shameful ways and will bring the way of truth into disrepute. In their greed these teachers will exploit you with stories they have made up. Their condemnation has long been hanging over them, and their destruction has not been sleeping.

2 Corinthians 11:3

But I am afraid that just as Eve was deceived by the serpent's cunning, your minds may somehow be led astray from your sincere and pure devotion to Christ.

Matthew 7:15–27

Watch out for false prophets. They come to you in sheep's clothing, but inwardly they are ferocious wolves. By their fruit you will recognize them. Do people pick grapes from thornbushes, or figs from thistles? Likewise every good tree bears good fruit, but a bad tree bears bad fruit. A good tree cannot bear bad fruit, and a bad tree cannot bear good fruit. Every tree that does not bear good fruit is cut down and thrown into the fire. Thus, by their fruit you will recognize them.

Not everyone who says to me, "Lord, Lord," will enter the kingdom of heaven, but only he who does the will of my Father who is in heaven. Many will say to me on that day, "Lord, Lord, did we not prophesy in your name, and in your name drive out demons and perform many miracles?" Then I will tell them plainly, "I never knew you. Away from me, you evildoers!"

Therefore everyone who hears these words of mine and puts them into practice is like a wise man who built his house on the rock. The rain came down, the streams rose, and the winds blew and beat against that house; yet it did not fall, because it had its foundation on the rock. But everyone who hears these words of mine and does not put them into practice is like a foolish man who built his house on sand. The rain came down, the streams rose, and the winds blew and beat against that house, and it fell with a great crash.

Life Changers

- Remember the H-A-L-T principle. It reminds us to avoid making any kind of big decision when we are either Hungry, Angry, Lonely, or Tired.
- Ask your pastor or youth leader to recommend a good book on how to identify cults and what to do when you encounter members of such groups.

Defending the Faith

Amy attends a large state university in the South. Right now she's sitting in a class called "Contemporary Sociological Problems." Moments ago the instructor made the statement that "there are no absolute answers to society's problems."

As a Bible-believing Christian Amy wants to object, but she isn't sure exactly what to say or how to say it. Her dilemma is compounded by the fact that the class has more than 100 students in it, including a good number of upperclassmen.

Amy's head is buzzing: *Do I wait and speak to the professor after class? Or should I raise my hand now? What if I say something and he ridicules me and my beliefs? On the other hand, maybe this is a chance for me to take a stand for Christ.*

As the lecture continues, Amy can feel her heart pounding. She begins to perspire. She wants to speak out, and yet she's scared to death. Looking at her watch, Amy realizes that the class will be over in a couple of minutes. *If I'm going to do something,* she reasons, *I've got to do it now!*

Thought Joggers

- What are the pros and cons of the options Amy is considering?

- How do you think you might respond in a similar situation? Why?
- When is it most difficult to take a stand for Christ? Why?
- What would be your answer to the statement that "there are no absolutes"?

Eye-Openers

Consider the practical advice about defending the faith found in each of the following passages:

1 Corinthians 2:1–5
When I came to you, brothers, I did not come with eloquence or superior wisdom as I proclaimed to you the testimony about God. For I resolved to know nothing while I was with you except Jesus Christ and him crucified. I came to you in weakness and fear, and with much trembling. My message and my preaching were not with wise and persuasive words, but with a demonstration of the Spirit's power, so that your faith might not rest on men's wisdom, but on God's power.

Colossians 4:5–6
Be wise in the way you act toward outsiders; make the most of every opportunity. Let your conversation be always full of grace, seasoned with salt, so that you may know how to answer everyone.

1 Peter 3:15
But in your hearts set apart Christ as Lord. Always be prepared to give an answer to everyone who asks you to give the reason for the hope that you have. But do this with gentleness and respect.

Life Changers

- Get with a friend and list several of the most common objections to Christianity.
- Pick one of the tougher questions from your list and try to come up with a biblical, concise, well-reasoned response.
- Ask your pastor or youth leader to recommend for you an understandable book on the subject of Christian apologetics.

Spiritual Smorgasbord

After completing the registration process at the beginning of her first semester of college, Shawn exits the doors of the Student Assembly Center. In front of her are dozens of clusters of people. Every student organization on campus (or so it seems) has a table set up.

Fraternities, sororities, service organizations, clubs, religious groups, even local businesses—they're all there, giving out smiles and greetings, brochures and flyers, free samples and coupons, lemonade and soft drinks.

Shawn begins to negotiate this gauntlet of groups, moving past the Skydiving Club and Beta Tau Kappa tables. She takes some coupons from a fast food booth, signs her name to a list of students interested in becoming involved with the Student Government Association, and then heads over to a row of tables in front of the campus bookstore.

She stops and stares. She counts. It's amazing . . . at least fourteen different tables representing the various Christian groups on campus. It's a whole variety of organizations—denominational groups, nondenominational groups, parachurch groups. She observes people laughing and talking together. She notices a few folks hugging friends they haven't seen since May. At one table are some guys playing guitar; at another are some people talking about the summer mission projects they've just returned from.

As Shawn is taking it all in, two guys run up to her. One says, "Hey, have you heard about The Fellowship? We meet on—"

The other student laughs and interrupts: "I saw her first! Before you visit *his* group, you've got to come to *our* meeting."

Shawn hasn't seen this many Christians her age in one place in all her life!

Thought Joggers

- What are some of the advantages for students who immediately get involved in a Christian organization at the start of their freshman year?
- What are some of the dangers for students who *don't* get involved in a Christian organization when they arrive on a college campus?
- What criteria should new students use to evaluate which groups they will attend?
- What group or church do you think you might attend when you get to college or move away from home and begin a new job?

Eye-Openers

When trying to select a church or Christian group, remember these principles:

2 Peter 3:18
But grow in the grace and knowledge of our Lord and Savior Jesus Christ. To him be glory both now and forever! Amen.

In other words: Get involved in a church or group that will help you grow spiritually.

Ephesians 4:11–12
It was he [God] who gave some to be apostles, some to be prophets, some to be evangelists, and some to be pastors and teachers, to prepare God's people for works of service, so that the body of Christ may be built up.

In other words: Get involved in a church or group that will equip you to serve.

1 Peter 4:10
Each one should use whatever gift he has received to serve others, faithfully administering God's grace in its various forms.

In other words: Get involved in a church or group where you can utilize your God-given abilities.

Life Changers

- Most colleges will give you a list of the various student organizations and religious groups that are active on their campuses. Write the dean of students at the college of your choice and request such a list.
- Ask your pastor or youth leader to recommend a good group or church in the town where you'll be living after graduation (assuming, of course, that you are moving away from home).